TIGER BAY AND THE DOCKS

THE STORY OF A REMARKABLE CORNER OF THE WORLD

TIGER BAY AND THE DOCKS

THE STORY OF A REMARKABLE CORNER OF THE WORLD

DAN O'NEILL

First published in Great Britain in 2001 by
The Breedon Books Publishing Company Limited
Breedon House, 3 The Parker Centre, Derby, DE21 4SZ.

ISBN 1 85983 230 X

Printed and bound by Butler & Tanner Ltd, Frome, Somerset
Jacket printing by GreenShires Ltd, Leicester

Contents

Introduction

FOR a boy savouring his green years, the Mystic East began at Cardiff's Clarence Bridge – opened a century or so ago, so local legend insists, by no less a celebrity than Jack the Ripper. Well, I believed it, anyway. In that sea-splashed slice of my city all things were possible.

A trolleybus ride across the River Taff took me to regions I thought of as remote and richly exotic as some Samarkand, as packed with adventure and intrigue as Bogart's seedy, sun-bleached Casablanca. I wouldn't have been surprised to see Bogey himself, smoke-shrouded as always, staring out from the window of the Ship and Pilot with the menacing Sidney Greenstreet and his simpering sidekick Peter Lorre just around the corner, maybe in the Packet. 'Here's lookin' at ya, Kid,' he would have said as he raised his glass. My penny trolley ticket, you see, was a passport to alien pastures.

The rest of respectable Wales might sleep as I paced forbidden streets (Mam thought I was at my Auntie Nellie's) but no one ever slept, it seemed to me, in this seductive corner of Cardiff.

These were the Docks, I wandered. This was Tiger Bay, I walked. In my fevered 14-year-old imagination Fu Manchu, prince of Oriental villains, lurked around the next corner, while opulent pleasure palaces for initiates waited behind drab doors supposedly opening on to disused warehouses. I knew better: each grimy street was transformed by my adolescent heat into alleyways as ominous as any in Macao.

Life with a capital L pulsed all around, and the chapel-heavy hills were far away. I look back, and realise that my image of the Docks and Tiger Bay owed much, too much, I now know, to the wilder shores of fiction. Yet I would discover when I returned years later, that often in this magical square mile or so, fact was often stranger than any fiction.

But my fiction-formed view of Tiger Bay was shared by so many others…

I remember a café. Look – look over there, by the window. Who else but the local Price of Darkness, the Bay's very own Fu Manchu. Imagine my awe as I gazed at the scarred cheek, the glittering eyes. Here's proof: a swarthy sidekick sidles in, short and sinuous, doubtless a Dacoit as read about in the Rover or Wizard, specially imported from the remoter regions of India. He whispers. What's this, I wonder? News of Tong warfare to come?

'Bloody 'Ell,' says Fu Manchu. 'Already?' And he leaves the café to disappear in the direction of the factory where Shirley Bassey will one day work, the factory where he operates a large guillotine that has nothing to do with gang warfare.

Naive? Of course I was. But that was the charm of the Docks and Tiger Bay: both inspired dreams.

Ladies of irreproachable virtue, housewives, shop assistants or schoolmarms, had only to stroll the dusk streets to be transformed by our inflamed young minds into veritable Mata Haris or, at the very least, those fabled ladies of the night who lured staid suburbanites to their doom. Inoffensive Chinese laundrymen, meek as sandalled mice, were transformed into Tong hatchetmen serving some local warlord. You'd see a curtain twitch and know beyond doubt that behind it were stairways leading down to torch-lit cellars where masked priests, oiled naked torsos gleaming, performed unspeakable rites to the beat of voodoo drums.

Wonderful, what a bootlegged bottle of light ale and a bit of wishful thinking can do when you're 14.

The enchantment didn't diminish as I grew older. The spell was always potent. On rugby international nights in days when Wales would *always* beat England on the old Arms Park, you were sure to find a brace of bemused Boyoes down from the Valleys, queasily recovering from pre-game celebrations that had made them miss the match. And of course, there were always the clammy-browed adventurers from the suburbs, Cyncoed or Canton, stuffed with stories of casual Bute Street customs that began where the *Kama Sutra* reluctantly left off. Clasping their pints they would stare uneasily around, and the girls in the corner of the Custom House would smirk, then advance, bleached barracudas closing in for the kill.

Yes, it happened, but behind it all was a community, multi-coloured, cosmopolitan, and as warm-hearted and closely-knit as any mining village. The buzz word these days is 'respect'. If you respected the people and traditions of the Bay you would find that warm heart – I outgrew thoughts of Fu Manchu as I outgrew dreams of Father Christmas. One of the most popular writers of the 20th century went down to Tiger Bay and, like me, was seduced by its spell. Listen to Howard Spring.

'Children of the strangest colours, fruits of frightful misalliances, staggered half-naked about the streets. And the shop windows were decorated with names that were an epitome of all the clans and classes under the sun. The flags of all nations fluttered on house fronts. It was a dirty, smelly, rotten and romantic district, an offence, and an inspiration.'

And then he added: 'I loved it.' Hopefully we shall find out why.

Before the Beginning

SO HOW did it all begin? What was the genesis of Cardiff's Dockland, and Tiger Bay, its twin?

Voice From the Back of the Hall (there's always one): 'Ask a stupid question. It started, of course, in October 1839, when they opened the West Bute Dock.'

Well, most historians would agree that this was indeed the date which saw the birth of what would become the greatest coal port in the world. But here's another question: just why did the Second Marquess of Bute risk his vast fortune on such a speculative enterprise? For the answer we have to go back a lot further than 1839: we go back 250 million years...

The branch of a tree slips into a swamp. Before any human being has ever walked this earth, the leaves of a towering fern are swallowed by a bog. Hundreds of millions of years on, that branch, those leaves, transmuted into coal, are scratched up in Bronze Age Wales, and used for cremation. A small start, the Docks and Tiger Bay still far off in the future. But by the middle of the 16th century we were burning over 200,000 tons a year. As the 19th century dawned we were producing ten million tons each year.

The birth of prosperity – but it's worth remembering, as we muse on a city literally carved from coal, what the true price was. Death was so

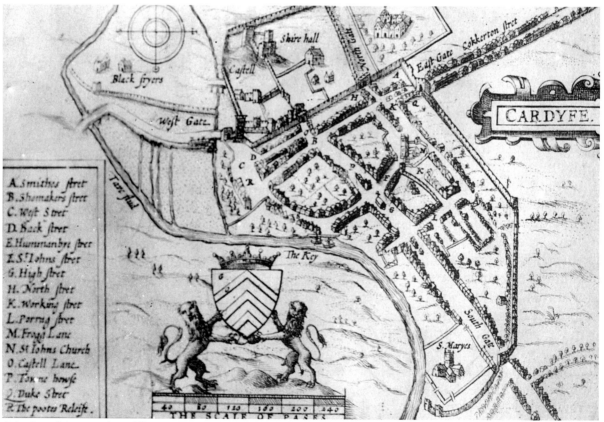

John Speede's map of Cardiff, 1610, tracing the original source of the River Taff. The crown above the shield shows where the Millennium Stadium now stands.

Quay Street in the 19th century, running down to what was the old Quay as seen on Speede's map.

frequent down there in earth's black bowels that a coroner's inquest was deemed unnecessary if the corpse was – and this is an authentic quote – 'only that of a collier'. Coal would also mean children as young as five toiling underground, some for 14 hours a day, dragging loaded tubs along roadways only 30 inches high.

All because of those trees, because of those immense ferns growing where tropical seas had lapped ancient shorelines when the world was young. That sea slipped back in a gradual great ebbing of the waters that could be timed only by the slow ticking of some cosmic clock, and as it retreated it was replaced by the deltas and steaming swamps that would determine the destinies of men and women as diverse as the Second Marquess and, odd thought, Shirley Bassey.

So in those deltas, around those swamps, lush vegetation flourished: giant tree-ferns and club mosses, colossal growths that were the first really substantial land forests. Over countless aeons the land-sea levels changed constantly and as seawater flowed in, so forests died, vegetation dropped and the deposits were compacted to form coal, to found fortunes and, in time, bring the West Dock and the streets and pubs of Tiger Bay.

But not yet. Not quite yet.

Think of shipping in Cardiff and yes, you see the docks in their pomp, vessels lining up in the Channel, literally queuing for places. But stand outside Cardiff's magnificent Millennium Stadium today and you are standing where the town's first true docks were built. For once, not all that long ago, the River Taff ran down what is now Westgate Street and here the Vikings sailed,

The banks of the Taff as Cardiff began to move into the industrial age, Penarth Head to the right in the mist.

leaving their echo in the name Womanby Street – Houndemanneby, the Huntsman's Dwelling – where they set up a trading post. Black Pagans, our ancestors called them, ferocious warriors led by men with names like Erik Bloodaxe and Sven Forkbeard.

And before them, did the noble Sir Lancelot sail this river, too? That's what legend says, adding that King Arthur himself and a force of 60,000 men followed him. Another tale out of the Celtic twilight suggests that it was along the Taff that Arthur was borne on his 'last, ill-fated journey'. Oh yes, Alfred the Great was spotted here as well: Tiger Bay has no monopoly on folklore.

A thousand years passes. And now you find the Town Quay (Quay Street), a wharf about 40 yards long, just up river from the Golate,leading to a smaller wharf half the size of the Old Quay.

Provisions for these wharves, quays and the protection of rivers were established by record of 1333, a later Royal Charter granted in 1531. The Marquess of Bute, then, was a latecomer and it's easy to imagine that those fans partying in the post-match pubs – on the corner of Golate itself – are surrounded by the shades of old salts. Yes, this really was the town's seafaring quarter in the 17th century. Vessels up to 200 tons sailed along – let's make it Westgate Street – sailed along Westgate

Street with 12 feet of water at the bottom of Quay Street at high tide. It cost a freeman of the town, one shilling (5p) to load his boat, half a crown to an outsider, and the cost was doubled if the boats were more than 60 tons.

And it's hard to believe, for those thousands who walk Westgate Street on the day of an international, that they are treading on the grave of a long-gone ship. For here, at the start of the 19th century, a barque turned over, spilling its crew into the water. You can imagine the consternation, the chaos, for this was the core of Cardiff's docks.

Along that river you'd find 13 wharves, 11 coalyards, a few tiny dry-docks, lumber yards and a lime kiln as well as all the traders inseparable from a maritime community.

A hint of the glorious future: here on the Taff estuary small vessels were loaded with coal hauled in by horse and wagon. This scene was drawn by Alexander Wilson 20 years before the first dock was opened.

Yes, a thriving little place. But Cardiff was on its way to becoming – oh, let's say it, it bears repetition – the world's greatest coal port. So soon there would be no place for the little moorings along the river bank where the ships collected coal to carry across the channel. Years earlier, from these same quays, they'd shipped out cannon for the British army fighting the American rebels – almost two centuries later the great docks would welcome some descendants of those rebels when the GIs trooped down the gang planks, finding themselves, incidentally, banned from setting foot

An unexpected find for these workmen digging on East Canal Wharf. They turned up this old cannon. Was this one destined for the British Army fighting the American rebels in the 18th century?

So by 1858 some contemporary commentator could observe: 'Quay Street now bears few traces of its former stir and bustle by the rough tars and plodding fishermen who used to navigate their crafts to the wharves.' River, then, would give way to rail. But there was a thread in the tapestry of docks and Tiger Bay; a thread just 25 miles long. It was called the Glamorganshire Canal.

The ironmasters of Merthyr had always shaken their heads over the cost of carrying their product down to the quays of Cardiff. As the 19th century neared, horses that must have been built like mastodons hauled wagons carrying astonishing two-ton loads along roads that had been massively improved since the General Turnpike Act of 1785. But this was a slow and costly method. So they decreed their mighty ditch from Merthyr to Cardiff, an engineering wonder that they thought would last forever.

It cost them £103,000 and to dig it they raised an army of mercenaries, men with muscles as hard as the iron itself, men who could hack out tons of earth and rock in the course of a single day. When a primitive form of conveyor belt was introduced two men could shift 1,400 barrowloads in a 12-hour shift 'for 18 pence a day.' This, we can say,

in what their commanders clearly regarded as too-tempting Tiger Bay.

All far off in the future, though, when the Town Corporation and Lord Bute combined to change the river's course. They had to, to accommodate the infant railway system which would become the biggest factor in the growth of the new docks and, of course, the area adjoining which would become Tiger Bay.

The approach to the West Dock soon after it opened.

The Bute East Dock in 1859. (Picture courtesy National Museum of Wales)

was the real start of the revolution that would bring the development of Cardiff Docks. Down the waterway, hauled by a single horse looked after by a man and a boy, down that waterway

The man who made it all possible – John, Second Marquess of Bute, the true founder of Cardiff.

they came, barges 60 feet long carrying as much as 25 tons. One man, one boy. It had taken 12 wagons to carry the same amount overland, needing 12 men, 12 boys and 48 horses. And now they went all the way down to the shoreline where a sea lock was opened, another seed from which the mighty docks would spring.

It opened in June 1798 and the first vessel through was the aptly-named Cardiff Castle, a sloop that had traded for years between the Town Quay and Bristol. It called for a celebration and the records show it got one.

'In June 1798, a naval procession took place, in celebration of the opening of the canal to the sea, attended by the firing of guns, and the ships in the harbour belonging to a few nations at peace with England, entering the basin with their respective flags flying.

A few nations at peace with England? Well, as Cardiff celebrated this opening to the sea, Napoleon Bonaparte was celebrating his conquest of Egypt, while ordering an expeditionary force to Ireland to aid the rebels there. My God, they must have been wondering, how long before Boney's fleet sails up our canal to Merthyr? Well, no Frenchmen went up the canal: but the coal came down in ever-increasing quantities.

In 1819 they carried 34,606 tons from Merthyr to Cardiff. Ten years later it was 83,729 tons. And in 1839, the Year of the Dock, no less than 211,214 tons. Cardiff was on its way. Yet only a couple of year earlier, in 1782, an unnamed Collector of Customs predicted that 'We have no coals exported from this port, or ever shall, as it would be too expensive to bring it down here from the internal part of the country.'

Not the kind of prophet to tip a Derby winner. Yet the very success of the coal industry spelled the beginning of the end for the Glamorganshire Canal. Lord Bute realised that its capacity was too limited for the ever-increasing tonnage being brought down from the valleys. And, as only small ships could enter the pond formed by the sea lock, he made the decision that would mean, a century on, his town (not yet a city) being renowned around the world as the home of – Tiger Bay.

He would build a dock.

And Bute Decrees
a Mighty Dock

HE DID. And his name is now synonymous with the seaport. But perhaps almost as much credit should go to another man of vision. For David Stuart, Bute's surveyor and engineer, wrote that 'If Cardiff is not made the greatest port in the Bristol Channel, it must be because Lord Bute does not choose to exercise his power.'

Bute listened. And chose to exercise his power.

As he owned much of the land around the Taff

The West Dock some ten years after it opened: the start of the surge towards greatness.

estuary as well as huge holdings in the coalfields it was really inevitable that he should build. But it was still a daunting gamble. Stuart surveyed the East Moor, an unappetising stretch remembered as 'a direful swamp... dangerous to traverse and of little value.' That would soon change. Bute went ahead. Stuart constructed a seawall and drained the land and here, in June 1835, began the excavations for the first of the great docks.

It would cost £350,000 to build, a colossal sum at the time and five times the original estimate. It took four years to complete and it opened, as the Bute West Dock, on 8 October 1839.

A damp and drizzle-licked start to the great day, rainslicked roofs shining in the tiny town of Cardiff. A day, you'd think, to lie abed. But this was a different day and who could lie in bed anyway when, at five o'clock, a series of shattering sounds (or 'thrilling blasts from the trumpets of the Glamorganshire Band,' according to Our Correspondent) erupted from the grounds of Cardiff Castle, scattering the snoozing seagulls, signalling to the citizens that wonders were on the way, that destiny was about to call. This, a writer

Three cheers for Lady Charlotte shouted the crowd. Was it for Lady Charlotte Guest, seen here as she was in 1842? Or for the ship entering harbour?

Where they celebrated the opening of that first great dock: the Cardiff Arms Hotel in 1890, the wall around the castle grounds just visible to the right. This would become the city's famous Animal Wall.

would observe a century later, this was the day on which Cardiff was truly born. And Our Correspondent from the *Glamorgan, Monmouth and Brecon Gazette* and *Merthyr Guardian* was there at the birth. Half an hour after the trumpet blasts he wrote, 'The streets were crowded, the merry bells of St John's pealing forth... we suppose every individual in Cardiff was stirring and heard the joyous noise.'

We can suppose that Our Correspondent supposed correctly. Hard not to stir with trumpets blaring and merry bells pealing, especially as almost everyone lived within earshot of the castle. But he caught the vibrant spirit of that morning as

Cardiff began its march to greatness. He had already been down to view the docks 'by virtue of my position' and he actually gasped, in print: 'A magnificent open basin 1,400 yards in length and 200 feet wide with room in its 18 acres for no fewer than 300 vessels.' And, he added, 'as thousands upon thousands of new arrivals have crammed into the town, filling every inn to overflowing, it ensures that anticipation is on the very tiptoe.'

Well, he's long since turned to dust, Our Correspondent, at one with Bute and Stuart and every one of those thousands upon thousands who came to Cardiff. But to read his words in an

A sad day in its history. Mourners line the shore as the body of the Second Marquess leaves the dock he had built, aboard the steamer Star. He died, aged 54, in 1848 and here we see the start of his last journey, first by sea to Bristol, then by rail to his resting place in Kirtling in Cambridgeshire.

old and brittle newspaper is to share his exuberance, to sense the air of expectation tingling through the town. Follow him that morning to the castle where he stands, pencil in hand, looking no doubt like an enthusiastic illustration from one of Mr Dickens' tales, *Oliver Twist*, perhaps, written the preceding year. And what he witnessed that day we see now, those far-away celebrations flickering on the mind's screen.

'At 7am the procession started from the Castle Grounds…'

Out of the gate and across to High Street. First, the 'mud labourers' (what gruesome task did *they* perform?), four deep, followed by the masons and the masons' labourers.

Then came the construction tradesmen under a flutter of flags and banners, before the band of the Oddfellows bounced brassily past. After them 'gentlemen and tradesmen of the town' followed by the Glamorganshire Band, whose trumpets had signalled the off.

His docks, pictured about the turn of the century.

Crowds still gathered to watch sailing ships scud away from the West Dock – these Cardiffians are there in 1905, the year when Wales beat the New Zealand All Blacks.

A view of the West Dock before World War One when ships waited days for a berth.

And who is this, pacing by in solitary splendour? An envoy from the Queen, perhaps? He looks dignified enough. But of course! It's Mr Stockdale, Superintendent of Police, brought down specially from London itself a year or so earlier to be the very first police chief of all. Behind him, the Sergeants at Mace and then, optimists all as they savoured the years ahead, the Corporation of Cardiff in all their frock-coated finery.

Easy to see the small boys scurrying through the crowd, then stopping to stare in awe – for here comes the man ranked just behind God and the

A vessel from Spillers steams out of the West Dock in 1913, the year when more coal than ever before cascaded down to the South Wales ports.

And some of the men who sailed them. A ship's crew in Cardiff posing for the unaccustomed camera in 1910.

Full circle: the West Dock Basin being filled in to form the site of the Maritime Museum. The tug Sea Alarm *ready to be set in cement as an exhibit showing what the dock once meant.*

Who could have guessed when they celebrated that night in the Cardiff Arms Hotel that one day their fine new dock would be no more than a watery playground for school kids. But here's this intrepid trio in August 1965, the dereliction behind them showing how the docks had declined.

Queen in the Cardiff pantheon. Yes, at the rear of the procession it's the Marquess, the Noble Lord. He nods to the throng as he treads his stately way, flanked by the Mayor, Mr Charles Croft Williams, and Lord James Stuart with, of course, footmen in attendance. Down High Street they marched and across the canal into Bute Street, Our Correspondent skipping along besides them, noting that 'Every window was thronged with elegantly-dressed females... flowers and evergreens everywhere.'

They must have marched at a rapid rate of knots for they were at the dockside in only three quarters of an hour, there to cheer the brig Lady Charlotte as she passed through the gate followed by the tugboat Glamorgan. The bands played *Rule Britannia* but there was no trouble among the crowd, noted Our Correspondent – 'Thanks to Mr Stockdale and his men.' Trouble? Remember this was the year when the country's rulers feared an armed uprising of workers inflamed by the Chartists. Until Chartist leaders were invited to watch the army's artillery in action, and muse on the effect it might have on them.

The weather brightened, the rain stopped, and in came the schooner *Celerity*, the yardarms manned and ablaze with bunting and banners. Then the highlight of the morning, 'the finest sight.' There she was, all the way from Quebec, the *Manulus*, a giant of 703 tons with 100 tons of timber aboard, proof that Cardiff was truly on the main sea roads.

For Alderman John Winstone, who could proudly boast as rugby supporters do these days that 'I Was There,' it was an emotional moment. When an old man, he recalled that 'The ship was decked with bunting from truck to deadeye, every yard manned as it came majestically down the drain.' He remembered the waiting crowd offering one huge cheer 'which was more than echoed by the sonorous huzzah from the yard arms.'

Our indefatigable Correspondent, busily eaves-dropping, heard several gents say they had never seen a dock like it, 'and as ship after ship appeared, so the cheers were given, while Lord Bute bowed repeatedly.' Drizzle swept down once more but it didn't stop Lady Charlotte Guest, wife of the great ironmaster, putting in, well, what else but a guest appearance. Instantly, wrote You Know Who, the cry went up: 'Three cheers for Lady Charlotte.' He added with a wink of his pen, 'For the Lady or the ship, I could not say.'

A great day then, ending, old Alderman Winstone tells us across the years, 'with pleasure in every heart and home.' The only dampener, apart from that drizzle, came when Lord Bute's carriage ran over the arm of an over-excited enthusiast stumbling into its path. But, recorded Our Correspondent, who clearly possessed the uncanny knack of being everywhere at once, 'The Noble Lord, immediately on hearing of the accident, with his accustomed benevolence of disposition, desired Mr Stockdale to see that every attention was paid to him.'

That evening in the Cardiff Arms Hotel across the road from the castle there was a grand dinner at which 300 noblemen and gentlemen and, of course, Our Correspondent sat down. It places things in proper historical perspective to hear again the first toast drunk to the sovereign. Raising his glass, the Mayor intoned: 'How

Another symbol of decline in 1963 with grass growing – as predicted – over railway tracks no longer used.

And now, it's 1968 and the dock begins to disappear, Bute's 'splendid and magnificent docks' turned into a dump.

fortunate that we have so fair, so young, so amiable a female wielding the sceptre.' Victoria, not yet 21, only two years on the Throne and two years away from wedding her beloved Albert, is seen through those words not as the white-capped old Widow of Windsor but as a slip of a girl.

Most of the evening was spent listening to speeches praising the man relentlessly described by Our Correspondent as the Noble Lord. Still, they were deserved. He had taken a huge risk to finance the work, mortgaging his undeveloped lands for half a million pounds. Between tributes, Mr Williams, the Mayor, delivered himself of a prophetic phrase.

'These splendid and magnificent docks will enable us to transport the treasures of our hills to foreign climes.' Sir John Guest added, with truth, that 'Few men could compute the advantages the town would deliver.'

Yes, world trade beckoned. But there were other, more immediate advantages. Before the coming of the dock the tides had swept in over land where Tiger Bay would rise, at times lapping up to the foot of Leckwith Hill on the fringe of today's city. The area that would become the Bay was all open fields, the cows grazing there being brought up to the middle of town for milking. Soon those fields would be no more as the sea town grew.

But on that October night those noblemen and gentlemen (and Our Correspondent) were there to celebrate the start of it all – they did, in traditional Welsh fashion. They sang *Of A Noble Race Was Shenkin* and the *Sicilian Mariner's Hymn* before giving the American Consul the last word, and a well-chosen word it was.

What cheers when he raised his glass to say: 'The dock will enhance the prosperity of Cardiff as long as grass grew and water ran.'

How the West Dock looked in the 1960s, the lock gates closed, the basin silting up, with Bute Street running down the centre of the picture to the Pier Head.

Who could foresee then that a time would come when yes, grass would grow over the dock itself... that small boys would paddle ramshackle rafts across its empty acres.

But that was how it all began. The arrival of *Manulus* ensured that in time a slice of the city would become enshrined in legend. Because of it we would witness the rise of a dozen buccaneering dynasties as the town took pride in the exploits of a breed of Rockefellers with Rhondda accents. Some of them, it was said, could scarcely read or write. But they could sign cheques for millions and they were always honoured – like those of the rich uncle from Texas, who signed his cheques with X's. Joining them would be men like Larry the Maltese and Donkey James; Bob Downey, King of the Bay, and the immortal Cap'n Tupper. Along would come Uncle Ike and Peta Link and coppers like Syd Adams whose fame spread to far-off Aden. And villains with names like Shanghai Walsh. All coming together to make Tiger Bay the most colourful, cosmopolitan corner of the country.

We're Posh – We Live in Loudoun Square

CLOSE your eyes. Imagine you are sitting in some dark cinema – let's make it the old Central, offering womb-like warmth on winter nights for the boys and girls of the Bay. The opening credits flicker. The camera rolls. And here's a sweeping view of the streets below. Here is Butetown today. But this is a dramatically different Butetown to the place once layered in legend. A streak of green traces the path of the old Glamorganshire Canal. And there are the docks, tranquil now, no clouds of coaldust hovering, instead a new cityscape rising, shining glass towers soaring where the great cranes crouched over countless coal-crammed holds. In the distance the familiar shape of Penarth Head is unchanged, unchanging, but the waters beneath it are no longer turbulent with tramp steamers or slapped by the paddles of pleasure boats

Portentous Voice Over: 'Today, the streets below are empty, the docks stripped bare of shipping, while the dockers and the Docksmen are departed.'

When this picture of Loudoun Square was taken in the 1960s, Miss Eliza Pincott and her Young Ladies' Seminary were long departed. But she and her girls would have recognised the place, changes were yet to come.

Then, what better echo of a time when this was the greatest coalport of all, the coaliest Klondyke the world has ever seen, what better reminder of times past than the Coal and Shipping Exchange, its great days gone, a monument, if you like, to Mammon.

Our screen fades. The images of modern Butetown vanish. Then, a babel of voices, a clatter of cranes, the roar of traffic and again, the Voice.

'But once these streets teemed with life while in that Coal Exchange vast fortunes were made in a single morning. For this (the Voice pauses for dramatic effect), this was the world's coal capital. This was... Tiger Bay.

And once more we see Bill Tatem, archetypal rags-to-riches tycoon, striding these streets on his way to a fortune, a Derby winner, and a title. Round the corner Shanghai Walsh and Larry the Maltese heave drugged seafaring men aboard ships bound for far-off places, that last spiked drink the ticket for a two-year trip. While all

The old Central Cinema where the girls and boys of the Bay found escape, long gone now like so much else.

And now, as the Square begins to disappear, one small boy, oblivious to time's passing, sits besides the little park where once Miss Eliza Pincott rested as the German bands played on drowsy summer afternoons.

Somali People's Restaurant and Sam On Yen's legendary Chop Suey House – all there only a few years ago along with ship brokers, coal factors, rope sellers, outfitters, laundries, dim speakeasies and discreet brothels, all there along with the ever-present pawnshop.

But all in the future as we trace the growth of Cardiff Docks.

Or that rows of bright new flats would rise where once lodging houses catering for every nation stood.

Yet for a while after the opening of that first dock it seemed to some that there might not be much future. The canal was often choked as the three hundred barges in use waited to pass through the locks, making the passage of coal and iron painfully slow. Trade in the new dock was pretty static – until the catalyst arrived in the shape of the Taff Vale Railway. There would be no looking back, for now the coal cascaded in torrents down from the Valleys. Black gold, they called it, but a better comparison might be with the oil that a century later would see the Emirs of the Gulf States as overwhelmed by sudden riches as Cardiff's coal and shipping kings, the Docksmen, had been.

By the 1850s they were hiring lookouts to bring news of approaching vessels. When the tip came, off they'd race to persuade bemused foreign skippers that theirs was the cargo worth carrying.

Could she ever have dreamed that one day massive tower block flats like this would rise above the square – the heart of Tiger Bay as the 1960s ended.

along Bute Street the cafes and the pubs pulsate, there's a rattle of dice on the pavements, the squawk of parrots outside houses, the sound of laughter from shaded doorways as old girls gossip and young girls giggle. And there's the Cuba café and the Ghana Club and the Rainbow Cafe; the

Enough of the end. Here's the beginning – the opening of the first section of the Bute East Dock in 1855.

One of them got news of an approaching Yankee clipper as he sat in the old Crockherbtown Theatre (the Park Hotel there now) listening to Jenny Lind, the fabled Swedish Nightingale. He rushed out in mid-trill, shouting for a cab. None in sight, so off he scurried to the Taff Vale Hotel where he hired a horse-drawn bus to gallop him to the docks. Imagine someone chartering a double-decker bus these days for a ten-minute trip. This was real competition. It had even been known for prominent Docksmen to battle bareknuckle over a ship, stripped to the waist on the foreshore. They fought over fortunes. At the other end of the scale men fought for pennies.

Port labour was mainly casual. Men turned up each day in the hope, too often the vain hope, that they might get a few hours work. They'd wait stoically on the quay until one or other of the foremen sauntered up to make his selection. Ben Tillett, general secretary of the dockers' union, spoke for those men when he described their treatment as degrading.

'A foreman or contractor walks up and down with the air of a dealer in a cattle market, picking and choosing from a crowd of men who, in their eagerness to obtain employment, trample each other underfoot, and where, like beasts they fight for the chance of a day's work.'

But as coal exports increased, aristocrats emerged: the trimmers, with their broad-bladed shovels, men who distributed the coal evenly in the ever-hungry holds. It was said of them that after each session in the Mount Stuart Hotel opposite the dock gates, the barmaids would sweep up half a hundredweight of coaldust with the sawdust. Once there were 2,700 of them, gone now, all gone – along with the Mount Stuart itself and the rowdy, raucous rumbustuous pubs of Tiger Bay.

Ah yes, Tiger Bay.

It began, believe it or not, as a somewhat staid settlement, the sort envisioned by Lord Bute when he planned the development of his docks. So up went the houses on land between the Glamorganshire Canal and the new railway servicing the West Dock. The older South Wales Railway running from east to west at the foot of what would become Bute Street would one day form a barrier between turbulent Tiger Bay and 'respectable' Cardiff. Although, in the mid-19th century sections of the town around, huddles of appalling housing like Landore Court or Mary

And the pile-up of shipping at that time that made the new dock essential – a forest of masts, no wonder one ship had to wait 24 days for a place.

But now, almost a century later, no ships wait, coal shipments are at an end, the end of the dock itself in sight.

Ann Street would be regarded with something approaching horror by the residents of Lord Bute's bright new homes.

He had planned a community to attract the merchants and sea captains, the traders and brokers and professional men, providing splendid housing in Loudoun Square and Mount Stuart Square with well laid-out terraces of smaller houses to the west of Bute Street. Mount Stuart Square began as a place of elegant town houses overlooking a central garden but over the years it would be transformed into the commercial centre of the docks and by 1886 those gardens would be gone, their space occupied by the Coal and Shipping Exchange, the heart of the docks.

But instead, let's look in on Loudoun Square, the heart of Tiger Bay. Let's visit on a day in 1858, three years after the opening of the Bute East Dock.

What's this? you're wondering. This crocodile of little Misses in bonnets and pinafores parading along the pavement? Well why not, why not when Miss Eliza Pincott supervises a Seminary for Young Ladies right here in the Square. While among her neighbours at number 8 is Mrs Cowell, teacher of French, the wife of Mr James Cowell, shipwright. In years to come French lessons will have a different connotation in the Bay but now, all around are the residences of master mariners and merchants, shipwrights and builders. The little park in the centre is a tranquil, tree-shaded refuge on the road from town to the docks, where sometimes you will hear a German band playing. Look carefully at the movie screen in your mind and there they are, Miss Pincott and Mrs Cowley,

sitting together on one of the ornamental benches, discussing the day's events, the wonders of the Royal Arcade built that year, or the opening up by Lord Bute of Sophia Gardens to the public.

The decay is reflected – like the building itself in the water – by the dereliction of what was once the Bute Warehouse, built in 1861 when the future of the East Dock seemed assured forever.

For the dockers, too, the great days are ending. These men wait in 1962 in hopes that they might get 'the call' for some work. Things don't seem to have changed much since Ben Tillett talked of 'a cattle market'.

Or talking, perhaps, of the terrible cruelties in distant India where the Great Mutiny has just ended, the awful massacre of Cawnpore still fresh in their memories, the images of slaughtered women and children so remote from their own well-ordered existence. Those men across the park, Docksmen perhaps, well they'll be talking about the the wonderful new vessel designed by the finest engineer of them all, Isambard Kingdom Brunel. His *Great Eastern,* the largest ship afloat, has completed her maiden voyage across the vast Atlantic, a wonderful omen for the future of the docks just down the road.

They were already building the Bute East Dock to be opened the following year, but as the port's prosperity blossomed, so did the aspirations of the people who lived in Loudoun Square. And there was enough money around to build fine homes in the new suburbs springing up, Llandaff a favoured destination, along with those to be built on Cathedral Road and Park Place as the Bay was left behind.

The names of the men and women who lived there so long ago were British. But successive street directories tell us more than who lived there and what they did. To go through them is like poring over a sort of municipal Dead Sea Scrolls, or as Schliemann did at Troy, uncovering, layer by

of an eminent Victorian shipbroker named John Greatrex. Twenty years later the building was a boarding house, proprietor Mr P. Andrianiko. In fact, this was one of 11 boarding houses in the Square that year, Miss Eliza Pincott's Seminary for Young Ladies now filled with former seamen who had settled, while where Mrs Cowell taught French you heard a dozen different languages.

As the old moved out, so the new moved in. Arab and African, Spaniard and Greek, West Indian and Maltese, a seasoning of old salts, you could say, who would build mosque and orthodox church and the white-spired Norwegian Church in the shadow of the twin towers of St Mary's, the

But the greatest of Tiger Bay landmarks still stands proudly on Bute Street – St Mary's Church, opened in 1842, and the twin towers financed by 'the ladies of the neighbourhood' through their bazaar in the castle.

And another view showing the High Altar and ornate carvings.

The interior of the church where the great and the good of old Tiger Bay worshipped.

oldest church of all. They'd started building St Mary's soon after the West Dock opened but in 1842 shortage of cash halted work on those twin towers – still a famous Tiger Bay landmark. More money was needed so, our old friend Alderman Winstone tells us, 'The ladies of the neighbourhood got up a bazaar for that purpose.' It was held in the dining room of the castle and consisted of six stalls. And, showing what a privileged place the future Tiger Bay held in their hearts, the cream of Cardiff society ran those stalls – 'Lady James Stuart, Lady Charlotte Guest, Miss Mary Stuart, Mrs Stacey and the Misses Homfray, of Llandaff.' A splendid marquee was erected in front of the castle with 'choice flowers, fruits etc., etc., sent from various gentlemen's establish-

layer, the past. For they speak of Cardiff's growth and the new Cardiffians who came from all around the globe, laying the foundations of Tiger Bay itself. They chart history. One example: in 1890, number 50 Loudoun Square was the home

ments.' It cost a shilling to go into the castle and you can bet that curious Cardiffians didn't hang back, given the chance to see how their lord and master lived. They flocked in, raising £600, an enormous sum – enough to finish the church towers, our Alderman rejoiced, 'leaving not a vestige of a debt behind.'

The church opened in 1842, Lord Bute among the congregation. He would live for five more years and in 1848 the body of the 'creator of Cardiff,' the man who built the first great dock, was carried aboard a ship to sail out of that dock. Thousands lined the shore to say farewell as the steam packet *Star* left the town. Bute's one-year-old son, the third Marquess, would become more famous for rebuilding Cardiff Castle and Castel Coch than creating docks

'Tiger Bay... Where You Get all the Murders'

THOSE ladies congratulating themselves on the success of their fund-raising could surely never have guessed the changes coming to their little parish. That 50 years on there would be 178 lodging houses in Tiger Bay including, of course, those in prestigious Loudoun Square. Or that in 1958, a century after Miss Pincott ushered her dainty charges across the road, her Square would be home to men and women with names like Silva and Da Cruz, Mohammed and Kaif and Saleh, Farrugia, Khalani and Khan.

But travel back to the time, make it the 1860s, when those boarding houses were first needed. For Cardiff was a port, *the* British port, to which seamen went after being discharged in, say, Liverpool or London. It was, said J. Havelock Wilson, general secretary of the seamen's union, 'the most undesirable port in the United Kingdom, the dumping ground of Europe.' The town was also regarded as the the worst port in the world for 'crimping' – crimps being those unsavoury characters who persuaded seamen to desert, hiding them until another sailing. They'd team up with the lodging housekeepers who would supply food and clothing, hanging on to the advance note for a month's pay the seaman had been given for a new voyage arranged by crimp or keeper.

Easy pickings for the crimps for, as Wilson put it, the shortage of cash was the sailors' own fault. As soon as they got their wages 'they guzzled their money away' and would sign on

The entrance to 'Sodom and Gomorrah' in 1890. Ladies of Bute Street gossip on the corner of Tiger Bay's best remembered road.

While almost 20 years earlier the first horse-drawn trams clatter down that road and here's how it started – the opening of the Cardiff Tramway Company's route from High Street to the Docks in July 1872. Different coloured discs were displayed on the front of the trams to announce the routes to those who could not read.

Bute Street in the Edwardian era. Were these the windows with a view worth ten golden sovereigns when the King came to Cardiff?

Looking down Bute Street towards the Packet Hotel (still there today) in the early years of the century.

The same section seen looking in the other direction, from opposite the Packet in 1982 when some buildings were restored.

at any rate to get a ship. The promise of instant cash from the crimps was enough and the profit came from cashing the note with the ship brokers after the vessel had sailed.

A report in 1884 recorded that 'the practice of harbouring and secreting deserters at Cardiff... has attained a magnitude at that port beyond any other in the United Kingdom. A ship is no sooner in the basin of the docks than she is infested by slop-sellers and boarding masters who go aboard in defiance of the ship's officers... the seamen are

But no restoration for this legendary landmark, the old Salvation Army Hostel which sheltered the homeless for generations. Still proud here, though, with desolation all around.

And two other buildings which are part of Docks's history. The main Post Office photographed in the 1890s and the Bute Street Post Office in the 1930s.

enticed ashore and shortly become the victims of the lawless and depraved crimps of the port and their associates.' This, really, was the beginning of the legend of Tiger Bay. But as seamen settled, married, became Cardiffians the flavour of the place changed as we saw with the departure of such solid Victorian citizens as John Greatrex. Bute Street was on its way to becoming one of the best-known (and notorious) thoroughfares in the world, the link – by horse-drawn trams introduced in 1872 – between 'town' and the docks.

But let's skip the years, let's leapfrog the strikes and the race riots and the the royal parade through Tiger Bay and the night they said farewell to Captain Scott and so much more. We'll come back to all that. So let's look at the Tiger Bay still remembered by so many old Cardiffians.

Tiger Bay!

You will not find it on any map ever printed. Nor does the name appear in any municipal directory. Even now people argue over just what streets actually formed the Bay. And there are just as many arguments over how it got its name. The files of the *South Wales Echo* suggest that some time in the 1860s – when crimping, you remember, was at its height – a small time concert party manager called Harry Moreton performed in Cardiff. One of the most popular songs in his repertoire was called *Tiger Bay* and the singer would slip a reference to Butetown into the verse. The name stuck and the rest, as they say, is history.

Or is it?

For the name's not unique to Cardiff. It's been used to describe other waterfronts. London and Guyana both had their Tiger Bays but who remembers them today? Tiger Bay still means Cardiff and although the vast new development in the city is called the Bay, for any true Cardiffian the word has a different, older meaning. Let's face it: no one is likely to write a series of thrillers about the new Bay, or make a movie or another TV soap (the last one bombed) based on the lives of the newcomers who have moved into a trans-

Bute Street nears its rumbustious end. Here it is in 1968 with demolition imminent – the twin towers of St Mary's in the background.

Nothing here to alarm that old lady who refused to leave the paddle steamer. This is 1995 with the new Bute Street risen, little houses replacing the famous cafés and pubs.

A 1996 look at that historic link between the docks and the town centre.

formed dockside. But they did about the old Bay.

And nothing so much sums up what those words Tiger Bay meant to Cardiff's staider citizens as the oft-told tale of the Old Lady and the Paddle Steamer.

She went down by bus from Cardiff to posh

And now a look at some of the most memorable pubs, starting with The Freemasons where the ladies of the night lived it up. Not so much a Free House as a free-for-all house.

Some of the regulars outside the Pembroke Castle in Louisa Street on a day with World War One just four years away.

Three children frozen forever outside the Anglesey Hotel in what looks like the year 1907 – surely those flags and decorations must be there to welcome Edward VII for the opening of the Queen's Dock.

Penarth one sunny summer morning for a stroll along the promenade. But she spotted a paddle steamer – one of the wonderful old White Funnel fleet – at the end of the pier. So off she went to Weston-super-Mare. That evening the boat returned to the Pier Head, Cardiff, the day trip over. The lady is supposed to have lived in Grangetown, a two-minute tram ride from the docks, but when she realised where she was she steadfastly refused to leave the steamer. 'This is Cardiff Docks,' she said. 'And down there is Tiger Bay, the place where you get all the murders. I'm not going.'

She didn't. She stayed aboard until the little steamer reached the safe haven of Penarth. Then she disembarked, catching a bus back to Cardiff rather than face the perils of Tiger Bay.

The Friendship Hotel.

And at the other end of Crichton Street, the Glendower, gone like the Custom House.

A dodgy pub to leave after a skinful – the Old Sea Lock right on the Canal Basin.

The Custom House on the corner of Bute Street and Crichton Street, favourite haunt of 'the girls' after the Freemasons vanished. Inevitably, it vanished in turn.

But the Packet's still there.

And here's its famous sign, Penarth Head behind that galloping steamer.

Caught by the camera in the room above his pub, Mr Smith, landlord of the White Swan Inn on Bute Street with the decorations up for the visit of the King.

It's unlikely that she would have attracted much attention. The White Slave Ring the local newspaper trumpeted of, telling lurid tales of young girls from the Valleys sold to brothels for as little as two bob, that fabled Ring wouldn't have been interested. In fact, women were offered as much respect around Cardiff Docks and Tiger Bay as in any other part of the city although outsiders brought up on the legend found this hard to believe.

Just a tuppenny tram ride, then, from those other places, those plusher parts of town. But as far as our old lady and her neighbours were concerned it might have been ten thousand miles away. Tiger Bay was as remote from Cardiff's posher suburbs as sinful Shanghai – and had earned the same sort of reputation. The very name was enough to send tremors down the spines of Valleys chapel-goers. While for the uninitiated the

prospect of a stroll along Bute Street must have been as alluring then as a midnight wander around New York's South Bronx might be today.

To them Bute Street was Sodom and Gommorah, awash with whisky, deep in drugs and streaming with scarlet women and brigands.

And yes, of course, there were predators there as in every seafaring town. Their main prey was that fabled beast, the Homeward Bounder, the sailor back from the sea but not in too much of a hurry to reach home and hearth without a bit of fun on the way. And as Cardiff had a reputation as a 'pay-off port' with hundreds of seamen leaving their ships carrying enticing wads, so the sharks gathered. You can see them now, sailors home from long trips, trooping exuberantly through the dock gates. A pint or two, perhaps, in the Packet or the Mount Stuart, then down to the Bay. There, if they were unlucky, to be rolled…

'Fancy a party, luv?' one of the girls would croon to the half-cut sailor celebrating his freedom after months of confinement at sea. It was an offer they couldn't refuse and it happened to a seaman they called Yank, ashore after a 15-month trip with a hundred quid in his pocker and a lot of leeway to make up. Yes, you've guessed it. There she was in a Bay pub, everything Yank had ever

The Crown, another Bute Street landmark across the road from the Custom House.

They built the Bosun to replace the great pubs that disappeared with the rest of Tiger Bay. But it didn't last.

The Paddle Steamer in, of all places Loudoun Square, did though. Astonishingly it's now the only pub in the area we called Tiger Bay.

dreamed of as he spent his 15 gruelling months at sea. He'd been saving his money, a shipmate later recalled, for a spree at home and here was the start of it.

That spree lasted only a couple of hours. Just long enough for Yank's new lady friend to get him drunk before summoning up some of the local muscle. Yank woke up bleeding in the gutter, relieved of his hard-earned roll, 15 months at sea for nothing.

'He didn't even go to the police about it,' said his shipmate. 'That's how they used to get away with it. The men they rolled knew they'd made fools of themselves and didn't want their families to know about it.'

That didn't happen a century ago. It was only in 1939. And the real tragedy is that Yank was killed on his next voyage when his ship, the *Tremoda*, went down with all hands.

Then there was Scottie, the sailor who never learned. His first stop was always the Freemasons, one of the best-known – and most infamous – pubs in the Bay. Every time he landed there he'd hit the bottle then go off with the same girl. And every time she robbed him. Finally Wally Towner, the landlord, said to Scottie: 'Give me your money and I'll look after it for you.' Scottie threw his bundle on the counter and got a fiver back for the night's expenses.

The next morning he turned up at the pub. 'She's robbed me again,' he said gloomily.

'No she hasn't Scottie,' said Mr Towner. And there was the money. 'You should have seen his face,' he recalled as he looked back down the years. 'He'd clean forgotten giving me his cash.'

Wally Towner had a lot of affection for those days just after the war.

'There were the girls, of course. They lived for the day. They'd make a lot of money and live it up, but some days they'd come in with black eyes. The pimps would give 'em those if they hadn't earned enough.' Tough times. Mr Towner kept an ancient bayonet by his bed, a shillelagh behind the

And here's a tribute to those old tycoons. Artist Frankie Locke at work on a banner in the Wharf, a huge pub built where the East Dock flourished. The painting shows some of the men who built the docks – those legendary 'Docksmen'.

bar. That bayonet, one police sergeant observed, was so rusty it would have given anyone blood poisoning – while the shillelagh was used 'now and then'.

It was needed.

'The girls used to quarrel at times but if I saw them at it I'd threaten to bar them and that would put the fear of God into them.' For the Freemasons, after all, was their office, their business premises. Once Mr Towner separated four of the girls 'clawing at each other.' He put two in the gents toilet, two in the ladies and told them not to come out until they'd finished scrapping. 'Said I'd give a bottle of wine to the winner.'

There were plenty of fights in the pubs 'and you just had to wade in and take a chance.' If the police were called they wouldn't bother too often with the lockup. 'They'd just take 'em round the back and give them a damn good hiding.'

Only the daftest, or the drunkest, would walk into a pub waving their pay about, bundles of those old white fivers. What a stir would ripple round the lounge. What knowing glances exchanged. Invariably the sailor would find company. Inevitably he would wake up next morning – skint. Even when there was no rolling it could be a dodgy business doing what the girls called business. Years before Scottie and Yank the girls of the Bay would wear long, pinafore-type dresses and sailor hats with large pins holding them on. If a sailor tried to short change one of them, why, out would come the stiletto-sized pin – and only the most foolhardy 'client' refused to cough up.

The girls were tolerated by most of the police all through the history of Tiger Bay but one famous copper of the twenties vowed to 'make

But it wasn't only pubs that offered a home from home for seamen. Here's the John Cory Sailors' and Soldiers' Rest in Bute Street, built in 1902.

Chris Brain, the brewery chairman, and the former Welsh Secretary David Hunt outside The Wharf on opening day in 1991.

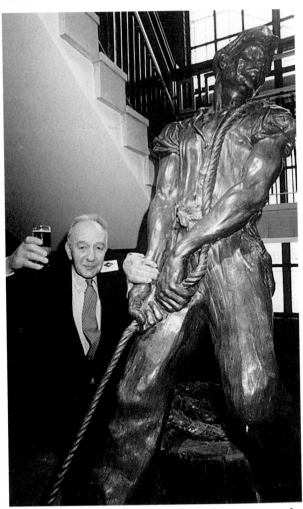

Inside, ex-docker Mattie O'Callaghan toasts the statue of a docker that's just about all that's left.

war' on the trade. 'I'm going to clean this place up,' proclaimed a detective called Gerry Broben, and in pursuit of this ambition he raided 80 brothels in a year. Nothing undercover about Gerry. He wore khaki breeches, leggings and a trilby hat just an inch or so short of becoming a sombrero, and one senior officer who worked under him as a young copper remembered him with some awe. 'He was a famous figure,' said Mr William Rees, later chief constable of Stockport. 'He quietened those Bute Street cafés all right. They were doing a roaring trade. A girl would give someone the glad eye and when they went upstairs another would take her place.'

An earlier, less impressive Rest.

And here's what those sailors found behind the carved façade: a floral hall looking like a palm court. This was taken in 1905 – yes, the year Wales beat the All Blacks.

Yes, Gerry Broben really was a famous figure. But only one among a gallery of famous figures.

Men like Syd Adams and much later Viv Brook, who was there at the death of old Tiger Bay, men who owned a different approach to law and order than today's police. It was summed up in the words of Inspector Ben Davies who ruled the Bay after World War One.

'There is more law in the end of my baton than in all the statutes of England,' he roared, and he spoke for every one of his men. Among them was the aforementioned Syd Adams, remembered by old timers as 'a bull of a man,' When Syd said 'Move,' men moved. So great was his renown that they whispered his name in such places as far off Aden: Syd Adams became a legend in the Arab world and all those legendary places 'east of Suez.' He was a typical Tiger Bay copper.

They were there when 54 nationalities lived in the Bay, among them 3,700 Africans, more non-white people than in all the country's other ports put together. But what's that? What about that White Slave Ring, as the local paper so luridly headlined its story.

Behind the sensation, a tragic little tale reflecting the darker side of Tiger Bay. Three seamen from what was then known as the Gold Coast and a 20-year-old Welsh woman were charged with procuring girls from the valleys as prostitutes. The girls weren't shipped abroad – as always happened in novels of the time featuring White Slavery – but some of them were handed over to the brothel-keepers of Bute Street for as little as two shillings. The judge the 'White Slavers' appeared before was suitably outraged.

'You have been engaged in one of the filthiest trades that human beings can engage in,' Mr Justice Charles thundered at them as they stood in the Glamorgan Assizes. Prison was the fate awaiting people 'who encompassed the ruin of young white girls.' Would his outrage have been so evident if the accused had encompassed the fate of young black girls? No one asked in those

This looks more like it. The games room in the Seamen's Institute, billiards and not snooker the choice.

distant days, but the fact that one of the girls was only 14 years old shocked everybody – and made the Bay's police more determined than ever to crack down on the pimps they hated.

Tiger Bay might have been a sin-filled slice of the city for the respectable ladies and gents of the outer suburbs and the valleys. But for their 'fallen' daughters it was regarded as a haven – perhaps a place where their fall from grace would be more easily accepted.

William Rees, reminiscing in retirement, suggested that in those between-the-wars years when pre-marital pregnancy was regarded as first step on the road to total ruin, young girls would run away from home to avoid the finger-pointing and end up in Cardiff. There, more often than not, they landed in Tiger Bay – as prostitutes.

'This was particularly true of girls from West Wales,' said Mr Rees. 'They couldn't live with the stigma of illegitimacy at home.' Yet often the established prostitutes would tell the police of any newcomers – Mr Rees never discovered whether this was to eliminate competition or sheer good heartedness. But it meant that often the police could trace girls who had run away from home and sometimes they would be welcomed back, saved from the pimps who prowled on the lookout for fresh goods.

As bad as the pimps were, there were other villains who might have strayed out of the pages of a Jack London seafaring novel – perhaps the nastiest predators of all. Among the least fondly remembered were a pair known as Shanghai Walsh and Larry the Maltese. They claimed they were a sort of employment agency, helping men get away to sea. Unfortunately the men they helped didn't know much about it until they woke up in some heaving focs'le 50 miles south of the Scillies, on that Road to Mandalay or, more likely, Australia or Argentina. It might have seemed a good idea to share a drink with this apparently pleasant pair – but drugs in the drink and an unscrupulous ship's captain desperate for crew invariably meant stormy weather ahead.

Shanghai Walsh and his cohort called their work Pier Head jumps and a very good living they made out of it But they'd long gone, and times were changing when Viv Brook started work in Tiger Bay as a young copper in 1950. For him it was a village, and he regarded himself as 'a village bobby.' There were good and bad people there, Viv recalled on the day he retired in 1985, 'but we could relate to them.' Even to the extent of carrying a husband up to bed if he'd drunk too much. to get him out of the way of his long-suffering wife. And talking of beds, how many coppers admit that they once shared one with a prostitute. It happened to Viv Brook.

While with the vice squad Viv, at one time a formidable front row forward, charged a door during a raid. No contest! His momentum took him straight through and on to the bed where a lady rejoicing in the name Big Rosie was already dispensing her favours to a startled seafaring man. There can never have been a more potent passion-killer. And he came across a lucrative little racket in Loudoun Square (shades of Miss Eliza Pincott and her Young Ladies) when he spotted a man running down the road carrying his trousers.

The runner helped, as they say, with Viv's enquiries which gave him another insight into Tiger Bay. 'Girls would wait for a John to start

Another monument to the Third Marquess who paid for it, the Sailors' Home on Stuart Street, seen here about half a century after it opened in 1856.

undressing then someone outside would yell 'Police raid' and off the customers would run, leaving the girls with the cash paid up front and no work to do.'

And then there were the boosters, the shop-lifters who ensured that you could buy just about anything at a knockdown price in the Bay. Viv was the man the locals called upon to retrieve their stolen property – after it had been moved on. He once knocked on a door while tracing a consignment of ladies' underwear that had been lifted when a voice from inside called 'Hold on Mr Brook, I'll just get these knickers off.' And out came the garments, one by one...

They called him 'Bullneck,' because, as one resident reflected, 'He was a big feller, always able to get on with it.' Suggesting that Viv, who retired as assistant chief constable, was in the tradition of Ben ('End of my Baton') Davies and Syd (Bull) Adams.

Viv remembered the pavement dice games, scenes straight out of *Guys and Dolls*, as the dice rattled and the pleas for 'naturals' echoed, and the panic when he appeared. The gamblers would vanish, leaving the stakes on the floor. He couldn't collect the cash himself, even if he took it straight back to the police station. Word would have spread: 'Mr Brook is grabbing the money.' So he would call the kids over – there were always

children hanging around a dice game – and they'd pick up the money and run.

But, as Viv discovered, 'When the gamblers got wise to this, they made sure it was their own kids who were ready to move in when the copper appeared.'

It was a different sort of policing where the rules could be, if you like, stretched. A copper could take a persistent nuisance around the back of the station and hand out a hiding with no comebacks from Above, Why? Well 'Above' would never know, although they'd have a pretty good idea of what went on.

Those Tiger Bay police were understanding, they knew what life was all about. A lad named

One of the Bay's legendary coppers, Viv Brook having a last look around his patch before retirement in 1985.

And here doing the work of a community bobby.

Johnnie Clifford worked for a bookie when he came out of the Merchant Navy at the end of the war, the classic 'runner' patrolling the pavements, taking the tanner bets before betting shops came to make it all legal. Being nicked was par for the course all over the city but when a Bay copper (not Viv Brook) came to collar Johnnie, well, let Johnnie tell the story...

'I told him I'd been away at sea for the duration of the war. All I was trying to do was to get some scratch to feed the kids. He asked me how many kids I had. I said five. So he just told me to carry on, and walked away.'

But always, over the years, there were places where seamen could relax in less – shall we say less exciting surroundings? Tycoons like John Cory set up homes for soldiers and sailors with a somewhat unexpected 'Floral Hall' inside – plus, of course, a billiard room. Cory's Floral Hall, you feel, could never really compete with the Freemasons Arms.

Well, Viv Brook called it a village. And so it was. But surely the most exotic village in Britain when Cardiff was at its shipping peak, when the future was assured and the death of the docks no more than a bad dream. Time then, to step back once more, back to a younger, more vibrant Cardiff, to a time when the docks were still growing. Back to the 19th century...

South Church Street, 1968.

Canal Parade.

Francis Street, taken from Canal Parade.

South William Street.

Herbert Street around 1955. Peerless Jim Driscoll lived in the house where the van is parked besides the lamppost.

Angelina Street, Loudoun Square in background.

Eleanor Street as the end approaches.

Eleanor Street School, Cardiff's first council school built in 1878.

Sophia Street ready for demolition.

Christina Street in 1965, the new towers of Tiger Bay showing the future.

Bute Place in 1957.

Even before the demolition men arrived Alice Street was starting to fall down by itself. These houses were collapsing but the residents were still houseproud enough to sweep up the debris.

It's 1963 and as the old houses around Sophia Street tumble, up goes the new in the shape of tower block flats in Loudoun Square.

Down go the dockland streets – Patrick Street being flattened here in May 1969, while Patricia Rees and her two small children wait for a move.

Bit by bit the Bay comes to an end, a lease of life for the Islamic Culture Centre but you wonder how that errand boy finds the right address.

Not much time left for the Pier Hotel which was at 84 Bute Street.

The bridge over the canal, turn right for the Bay, Custom House Street ahead.

A flower seller outside the Docks Post Office at the turn of the century.

Happier times: Mount Stuart Square in the 1930s, looking across James Street to Penarth Head.

And this is how it was in 1927. James Street runs through the centre of the picture towards the swing bridge over the canal with the River Taff to the extreme left. All the houses have long since been flattened. Powell Duffryn House in the bottom right hand corner was replaced by the Welsh Industrial Museum, itself now gone.

And here's Powell Duffryn House, formerly the Merchants' Exchange, in its prime.

Blood on the Streets of Cardiff

AT THE start of the 1880s, so vast was the volume of coal being ripped out of the Rhondda and surrounding valleys, even Bute's fine new docks couldn't cope. They were in real danger of grinding to a halt as there was no room for storage in the narrow valleys, no space for huge sidings so only about half the ships steaming in could be loaded on the day they arrived. So congested were the rails running down to the docks that it could take nine hours for the coal-crammed wagons to get from Pontypridd to Cardiff – some 20 miles. Train drivers reported that it was not uncommon to spend an entire eight-hour shift on the line without moving.

Another dock was needed.

To help build it the docks authorities levied an additional penny a ton on the coal, believing that as there was no real alternative anyone using the docks would have to pay up. But not David Davies, great railwayman and opener up of mines.

He'd be damned if he'd pay the Marquess of Bute a halfpenny a ton for use of his sidings, another halfpenny for shunting charges. He would bypass Cardiff Docks, he vowed. He'd drive a new railway line out of the Rhondda to an outlet in the hitherto sleepy town of Barry.

'We have five million tons of coal,' he snapped, 'and we can fill a thundering good dock the first day we open it.' And before he finished his fight, he vowed, 'grass will grow in the streets of Cardiff.'

Well, Davies built his docks and Barry, with a population of only 478 in 1881, would be a world-renowned port 40 years later when, for a brief and glorious moment, it actually overtook Cardiff in exports. But grass didn't grow on the streets of Cardiff: Neale and West trawlers, the city's own fishing fleet began operating and Cardiff was in the news, as well, when the Welsh sailing ship *Merioneth* broke all records by sailing from Cardiff

It seems so peaceful as we look south from the Pier Head in 1864 but soon those paddle steamer tugs will be in action for the ships were coming to the docks around the corner in ever increasing numbers.

to San Francisco, round the Horn, in just 96 days. All this and the opening of the Roath Dock in 1887 (Bute himself, operating a huge mechanical 'navvy' ceremonially started the work), made David Davies's threat look a little hollow. But his wasn't the only threat to the tycoons of the time as they celebrated ever-increasing profits. The men who brought them those profits wanted a share – and to get it they formed the National Amalgamated Labourers' Union, effectively banding the dockworkers together to go with the Cardiff Coal Trimmers Union.

In Bute, though, they found an uncompromising opponent. Ben Tillett, of the dockers' union, wrote that Cardiff was 'the only port of any importance in the United Kingdom where employers had refused to meet men as represented by their trades unions.'

So on 4 February 1891, the first great strike in

A panoramic view in the same year of the Bute Docks.

the history of Cardiff's docks began when the coal-tippers, the men who loaded the ships with coal, downed tools. It swiftly became a fight for the basic principles of trade unionism, in effect,

One of those paddle steamer tugs towing a vessel out of the Bute Docks.

'Grass will grow on the streets of Cardiff,' said David Davies, before he would pay to use Bute's docks. Instead, he built his own in Barry.

And here's his statue outside the Barry Dock offices, targeted by birds...

JOHN III MARQUESS OF BUTE   EARL OF WINDSOR

...just like the pigeon-spattered statue of his old enemy the Third Marquess of Bute in Cardiff's civic centre.

war was declared between Docksman and docker, and we would see armed police on the streets of Cardiff, bringing battles and bloodshed.

It lasted just six weeks – but they were weeks which would burn their way into Cardiff's psyche. And the dock workers swiftly saw how much influence the Docksmen and their allies owned. What else, when they could bring police

The Third Marquess begins the work on his new Roath Dock by starting up a 'steam navvy' in February 1883 to the cheers of labourers and the VIP's in the stand.

A close-up of the great man in one of his dry docks.

And some of the men who worked those docks – these are at the Junction Dry Dock probably in the 1890s.

from well outside the town into Cardiff, police, moreover with sidearms 'prominently displayed' as they marched from the station. It had begun as a traditional protest by workers who felt they deserved more reward for their investment of muscle into the vast profits being made by the ship-owners and coal tycoons.

But as soon as those coal-tippers downed tools 'scab' labour was brought in to work the tips and the employers even ran a special train down from Liverpool packed with strike-breakers – a reflection of the

It's 1887 and here's the flag-bedecked SS Ninian Stuart *breaking the ribbon for the opening of the Roath Dock.*

Who could have predicted then that in time ships would have to 'double-park' so busy would the Roath Dock become.

Or that huge vessels like the liner Victoria would be fitted out in the Roath Basin.

way in which America's 'Robber Barons' had enlisted private armies to smash protest over there. Cardiff's dockers were so incensed that to avoid possible trouble police were imported from England to keep order. At one time the local police force was supplemented by 140 extra men – 40 from Glamorganshire, the rest from Gloucestershire, Staffordshire and Monmouthshire. It was the Staffordshire Police who marched from the General Station with those guns on daunting view. They were on their way to the Grand Hotel where they were billeted, living in luxury, the strikers hinted darkly, while they were on starvation money.

To the workers they were an occupying army but warnings from strike leaders to steer clear of trouble were obeyed. Yet some were charged with assault and one leader was accused of intimidation although contemporary accounts suggest that there was plenty of provocation – reminiscent, perhaps, of the actions of some 'outside' police brought in during the great coal strikes almost a century later.

A familiar sight during the days when Coal was King and the marshalling yards were always filled.

While massive cranes would be brought in to load iron plates in days when the foundries of Wales never ceased flaring.

But here a portent of the end as the Roath Dock, from which so many millions of tons had gone, sees American coal being delivered during the miners' strike of 1972.

A seaman called Moffatt returned to the union headquarters bleeding from a gash on the head, claiming that two policemen had followed him down Bute Street before kicking him to the ground and hitting him with their batons. He'd hardly finished complaining when a third striker turned up protesting at being beaten by police. He was followed by another with a dislocated shoulder after being set upon by the 'foreign' police.

John Gardner, secretary of the National Sailors and Firemen's Union, wrote to the Cardiff Watch Committee asking them to halt the provocation – summed up in the words of Superintendent Tamblyn, the police's commanding officer, after a visit to strike leaders.

'The next time I come to this place it will be to draw blood from some of you.' He also challenged the strikers to go out into the street where he and his men 'would give them fighting enough.'

The Watch Committee held an inquiry, considered the complaints, then, to no one's surprise, dismissed them as unproven. They did suggest, though, that Tamblyn should keep his men's tempers cool 'at so heated a time.' The strikers had been told from the start to be 'orderly and decorous' in their behaviour, particularly during a huge demonstration on 1 March, St David's Day, when 10,000 men marched through the streets of Cardiff. They were led in eye-catching fashion by a man on white charger and the parade concluded without incident, the police simply offering a baleful presence. There was no intimidation this time, perhaps because the public seemed to be on the side of the 900 strikers, donating large amounts of cash to reinforce the one pound a week that replaced their wages.

There had already been other mass meetings and a week before the big St David's Day event the strikers marched down to the docks headed by their specially-formed fife-and-drum band, banners fluttering. They sang such rousing ditties as *Hark! The Battle Cry Is Raising* and, to the tune of *Hearts of Oak*:

'Firm and fast we shall stand, Heart to heart, hand in hand, In fair or foul weather – Brothers together, A people united to be free.'

They were ready, they proclaimed, for a fight to the finish. But they went back to work on 14 March with newspapers, who had almost all supported the employers, gloating that 'they had been beaten all the way round.' A union official, unwilling to admit total defeat, conceded that 'the strike was not as successful as we would have desired it to be.'

While Ben Tillett, one of the great men in the history of trade unionism, claimed that 'defeats often spell victory, because they make us aware of our points of weaknesses.'

A local trade union leader was probably closer to the truth: 'At least,' he said bitterly, 'we now know who our friends are.'

Seven years later the miners of South Wales struck against proposed pay cuts and once again the troops were moved into South Wales. Even one of the mightiest coal-owners of them all, D.A. Thomas, the future Lord Rhondda known as 'The Czar of the Coalfield' couldn't stomach it. He demanded action from the Home Secretary telling that minister that soldiers stationed in Mountain Ash 'became intoxicated and created disturbances in the streets, ladies were grossly insulted and many free fights took place.' When you consider that one miner's take home pay from the Albion (Cilfynydd) Colliery four years later was all of 6s 6d (32p) a week you can understand the men's feelings. Ah yes, the miner, one Noah Jones, did have his rent of 6s 3d plus 6d a week for the accident fund taken out, but that would still make his gross weekly pay less than £1. The following year when the price of coal dropped by 2s a ton, Noah Jones would be forced to take another ten per cent pay cut...

The Cardiff dockers could sympathise: they had been through it, and, what's more, they were linked almost umbilically to the miners who sent down that black gold. But the workers were flexing their muscles, ensuring that there would be other, much more catastrophic strikes, the next big one in 1911. This would introduce us to the immortal Cap'n Tupper, a man who could have given Hitler himself lessons in inflaming the mob – and in using another race as scapegoat as well. But first, let's look at the years leading up to the building of the next dock, and some of the odd events that filled them.

Rising Sun Meets Red Ensign

'BUT it was just such a morning, a hundred years ago, That the Pier Head it was wreathed in smoke, And men died down below.'

A couple of lines from a monologue by a Cardiff folk singer, Tom Fletcher. They recalled the great disaster that struck the town's docks on a morning in March 1886. Today we define a disaster as, say, a jumbo jet crashing into a crowded hospital, or one packed train smashing its way into another. A two-car crash with six killed is now just another run-of-the-mill accident.

So it's a measure of the relative tranquility of the times that we still remember the impact on Cardiff's consciousness of just six deaths in that year so far distant that Coca Cola had just been invented, the year when the Statue of Liberty was raised in New York, when the great Apache war chief Geronimo surrendered to the US cavalry. In Cardiff the explosion that shattered the steam paddle tug overshadowed all these events – but when you think about it, why not? After all, these were Bute's great docks, destined to be the (let's

The wreckage of The Rifleman *in 1886. Perhaps one of the paddle steamer tugs seen in other photographs.*

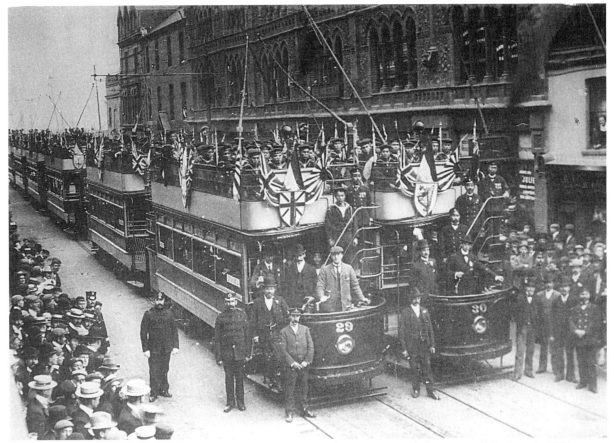

Cardiffians turn out on Bute Street to gape at the strange visitors from Japan, ready for a tour of the town in 1902.

say it again) the World's Greatest Coal Port and they were central to almost everyone's existence.

The people who worked on those docks, the trimmers and the dockers, the boilermakers and the pilots and the clerks and most of the tycoons were local. And so were the men aboard the 60-ton Rifleman. It was the oldest tug registered in Cardiff Docks, owned by Mrs Speir of the Museum Hotel, South William Street. And at nine o'clock it waited to take out a vessel called the *Eleanor Edith*, its crew sitting around the boiler eating breakfast.

Then the boiler blew up.

'The boiler plates red hot and then, cold water left to run, Her safety valves screwed down too tight, Six families' lives undone.'

The captain was Henry Pill a married man of 30 with five young children, and according to reports of the time he was blown 'clean over the old clock tower.' His mate William Henry Gerrish, the same age, father of two, died with him. John Lovell left five children fatherless and 19-year-old John Clare died instantly. The captain's brother-in-law, 'a boy named Phillips,' died the following day.

So what about the sixth death mentioned in the song? Well, William Hunt, a dock pilot, was on the deck of an Italian barque, the *Clothilde* in the Bute East Basin when a chance in a million killed him. A chunk of the *Rifleman's* boiler weighing four and a half tons sailed 250 yards through the air, landing in the *Clothilde's* rigging before smashing down on Hunt. James A. Sweeney, standing near Hunt, was luckier. 'I escaped without any hurt,' he told reporters, 'but my hat was damaged by a piece of falling debris.' These days he'd claim compensation! Two other seamen were injured and taken to the Hamadryad Hospital and yet more chaos was caused by the horses pulling one of the legendary Solly

Later they take part in a regatta, again watched by curious crowds and men from their ship.

Andrews' buses at the Pier Head. They were so terrified they backed into the windows of a coffee shop – emptied of customers who had all rushed to the dockside to gaze ghoulishly down at the wreck.

The monologue, supposed to be delivered by the sad shade of William Hunt a century after his death, ends:

'*Nothing moves except for one old dredger in the roads, Where a hundred years ago a hundred ships would wait for loads.*'

Which pretty well summed up the docks in 1986 as they gently decayed, waiting for the next period in their history. Of which more later.

Well, the *Rifleman* caused a sensation. But it was a tragedy that the people of Tiger Bay and the Docks could accept. With it, they were on familiar ground – or maybe water. Imagine, though, their feelings when representatives from what was then probably the most isolated country on earth, give

or take a Tibet or two, came to town. For years the photograph of these mysterious tourists baffled us and the question most asked was: What on earth are these weird visitors doing packed into tramcars in familiar old Bute Crescent?

They might have been Martians, these 'smart and sturdy little visitors' to South Wales in the summer of 1902. They were strange even to the Cardiffians thronging the pavements. Those men in bowlers and straw hats were accustomed to seeing Chinese and Arab and African around the dockland streets. But these were different. These were Japanese.

Why were they here? You find the answer again, in faded old cuttings. These were sailors from the battleship *Asama* and its accompanying cruiser *Takasaga*. They sailed up the Bristol Channel and as soon as their steam was sighted thousands of curious locals filled Nells Point at Barry Island and packed the paths along the Penarth clifftops – in much the same manner as their great grandchildren might today turn out to gape at an arriving flying saucer. These Japanese were just as alien as any visitor from outer space. As the ships approached the docks hundreds of men and boys – not many women in the photograph – hurried down to see this strange new breed of sailor. The *South Wales Echo*, perhaps a shade patronisingly, called them 'Jap Tars,' while reporting that the Mayor of Cardiff had hastily arranged a Town Hall lunch for Admiral Ijuin and his officers.

South Wales put out the flags, including, of course, the Rising Sun, and the town's 'private citizens' arranged a lunch for the crew in the Park Hall (not the Park Hotel). This could be the destination of the sailors in our tram cars, who look as though they regard those spectators gazing up at them as a species as exotic as the spectators found them.

Members of the crew went to Merthyr and visited coalmines and on the Saturday before sailing away they took part in the Penarth Regatta,

And here they are lined up on the deck of the cruiser Takasaga...

...before sailing out past the Bute Dry Dock.

crews from the *Takasaga* rowing against each other for a first prize of £5.

The *Echo's* Man About Town attempted an interview with an accommodating Jap Tar but made the unfortunate salt sound like the late Benny Hill doing his Chinese impersonation: 'Ca-har-dar velly inneress-ah...' The Japanese, in keeping with the secrecy that surrounded their homeland, weren't allowed unrestricted shore leave. It would have been velly inneress-ah to see what the reaction might have been had they encountered Tiger Bay's legendary ladies of the night and their protectors. Still, while in the Bay they could have got beer for only 3d a pint.

The 'smart and sturdy appearance of the

visitors was the subject of general comment,' the *Echo* announced while a special article was headlined 'Our Friend the Jap,' informing readers that 'The Japanese bluejacket is a charming man.'

All a bit patronising, with our indefatigable Man About Town airily telling his captive Japanese audience that the British Navy was the world's best. But only three years later some of these Jap Tars were doubtless part of the Japanese fleet that smashed the Russian navy to show, for the first time, that an Asiatic power could master a European nation and that the balance of world power had changed forever. And in 1942 other Jap Tars would be in thunderous charge of vast areas of the Pacific after their mighty aircraft carriers had helped demolish Pearl Harbor.

But no bowler-topped gent or clerk in straw hat, not one of those spellbound spectators captured by a camera on that docks street so long ago would have believed it.

To them it was just another day in the often bizarre history of the Docks and Tiger Bay. And there were so many. Meanwhile the Docks were approaching their greatest period, the King was on his way to Tiger Bay, and the men who made their millions from coal would discover the true cost as an entire community died as though blasted by an atom bomb.

Looking over Tiger Bay a century ago, and note the canal packed with barges.

The docks showing the post-war rundown.

But in 1880 you could catch a paddle steamer like this one, Success, every 20 minutes to Penarth.

The Bute Docks in 1891.

Spiller's great flour mills at their peak.

Building the Graving Dock mainly by muscle-power in 1883.

And using that dock to repair the Lizzie, part steam, part sail, in the 1890s.

And not long after the start of the mills when horses provided the transport.

The Roath Dock, just before World War One.

Docks warehouses around 1890.

Early days: a tea clipper alongside in Cardiff docks.

This is how it was in the beginning – a forest of masts with more lining up in the Channel.

Another glimpse of the great days.

And it's all go as the little tugs tow in yet more vessels.

Leaving the docks after a refit, the Hannibal, *possibly a warship.*

Sail and steam mingle at the docks between the wars.

Sugar beet is sent out by conveyor belt to waiting railway wagons.

The entrance to Bute Docks in two different eras.

Another delivery, this time New Zealand butter in 1939 – before it was rationed.

A curious crowd gathers in 1912 to watch the docks very own floating fire engine in action.

It's 1952 and the grass is beginning to grow.

So what happened to our docks? The South Glamorgan County headquarters looking over the empty dock where once we had ships.

Coal no longer leaves the docks – instead fruit comes in. And here's an inflatable building, the first in any British port, to be used as a transit shed for the increasing tonnage of fruit coming through the docks. It was 250 feet long and 60 feet high. Cost: £20,000 in 1971.

The End is Nigh: plenty of room in Bute's old docks where once ships double parked.

The Pier Head Building all lit up to celebrate in 1989 the 150th anniversary of the opening of the West Dock.

Derelict berths facing Penarth

But Cardiff now looks to the future – and here's how they were building it. Work on the Barrage with that Pier Head building over there in the distance, showing the scale of the operation.

And to finish – an impression of how Tiger Bay and the docks will look in the 21st century. Bute Street, looking north.

He's Jack the Ripper – He's Got a Top Hat

THE first great strike had been over for just six months when Jack the Ripper came to the Docks and Tiger Bay. Or maybe we should say the man plenty of people *thought* was Jack the Ripper. While adding that some still do, although this could be as bizarre a conspiracy theory as saying that John F. Kennedy was murdered by Martians.

Still, you can imagine some awed local saying, 'But he was wearing a top hat. And we all know the Ripper wears a top hat...'

Well, the blood-chilling Ripper murders were still fresh in the minds of Cardiffians in 1890. For only two years earlier, in those few months of 1888 which have gone down in criminal history as the 'Autumn of Terror', the most celebrated serial killer of the century stalked the fog-shrouded alleyways of London's East End. He killed and

horribly mutilated at least six prostitutes and his immortality is ensured because the true identity of the killer known as Jack the Ripper has never been conclusively proven. Plays, films and books have placed his image firmly into the public psyche: the name conjures up visions of a shadowy figure of almost supernatural cunning moving menacingly through the vice-infested back streets of Victorian London – and indeed, some students of this man who became forever the archetypal serial killer suggest that there really was something supernatural about him.

He vanished at the end of 1888 and some say he went to America where he continued his killing. Others insist he committed suicide. While

Togged up in top hat and tails the Duke of Clarence opens the bridge across the Taff named after him. It's 1890 and Jack the Ripper has never been caught. Is this him? Some historians still wonder.

Just up the road from the ceremonies women unload potatoes, back-breaking work which earned them paltry pay.

Children play on the river bank as the bridge is being built.

one faction maintains he was caught and, because of his high position, was placed in an asylum where he died years later.

And, of course, there are those who claim that he came to Cardiff in 1890 to open the bridge that in turn opened up yet another route to the docks.

All very melodramatic, but if you're looking for real sensation, why, what better suspect than the second in line for the throne, the grandson of Queen Victoria, the son of the heir himself, the Prince of Wales? And there he stands, top-hatted and tail-coated in the centre of the picture commemorating the day, Cardiff's bearded mayor looking up at him as the ribbon prepares to be snipped – Prince Albert Victor Christian Edward, Duke of Clarence and Avondale, already suffering from syphilis, presumed bi-sexual, with an IQ said to be lower than his hat size. Those who see Eddie as the Ripper suggest that the killings were in revenge for the disease he'd contracted as a cruising youth in the East End or had been arranged because he'd fathered a child and the Catholic mother, said to have been secretly married to the Prince, had to go – the other unfortunate victims being chosen simply to avoid revealing the real target. At that time the news that the heir but one to the throne had married a Catholic girl would have opened up a can of constitutional worms that could have ended the Monarchy

The theory is that once Buckingham Palace realised what Eddie was up to they placed him under the supervision of the royal physician William Gull until he died of pneumonia in 1892. Another theory is that Gull either finished Eddie off himself or supervised his 'euthanasia' because, whether he was the Ripper or not, he was too big a dim-witted liability to be allowed to live and become King after the death of his father, who himself was crowned Edward VII in 1901, ruling until 1910.

Instead his younger brother inherited his position along with his fiancée Princess Mary of Teck, going on to become George V with Mary as the strait-laced Queen Mary, grandma of Queen Elizabeth II.

Whew, after all that it's a relief to get back to normality on what was, after all, a great day for Cardiff. Although,looking at that ancient photograph you can still get a pleasant thrill out of wondering whether...

But, back to that normality which, incidentally at that time, included women – mothers of children like Jim Driscoll – unloading potatoes down at docks, back-breaking labour throughout the day for workhouse pay.

Anyway, in 1889 there was only one bridge crossing the river near the Taff estuary and it was owned by the Taff Vale Railway. In 1886 the company decided to charge a toll. The toll gate was swiftly demolished by angry workers whose only route to the docks from Grangetown was over this bridge but the company refused to remove the tolls when urged by the town council. So the radical Mayor of Cardiff, Alderman William Sanders, suggested building a new bridge across the river with another smaller one over the Glamorganshire Canal.

This meant a much-needed new entry to the docks from the west of the town and a magnificent bridge was planned, a huge iron structure looking in that old picture like something constructed with a giant meccano set, its central span weighing 500 tons, able to be swung right round by four men in five minutes allowing ships to pass under.

For years small boys in Grangetown and the Docks believed that untold numbers of workers had plunged from the bridge during construction – to be lost forever in the thick, oozing mud left by the Taff's tremendous tidal race. Just more

While a picture from another angle shows the mud which small boys believed swallowed dozens of workmen.

small boys' romancing, it seems, but this was truly a triumph of engineering and only a significant top celebrity was deemed fit to open such a splendid structure. So, on 17 September 1890, the 26-year-old Prince Eddie came to town.

They were roasting oxen in Mount Stuart Square, bands playing and flags flying, the streets crowded, the pubs packed with the whole town a-buzz for this first royal visit. No tabloid revelations in those distant days so the visitor was treated like, well, like royalty. People climbed up lampposts, clambered on to roofs and railway coaches to glimpse this exotic being and others paid 7s 6d for seats on specially-erected platforms along the banner-bedecked route he'd take. There was a free feast for 1,200 people with treats for the children and a firework display as families flooded into town from all round. Eddie arrived in a special train, stepping out to be described by an *Echo* reporter as 'a tall Englishman with a top hat, a long frock coat with the top button negligently unfastened, and a broad white tie with a glittering diamond pin.'

Four grey horses pulled his carriage through the streets and outside the castle was a facsimile of the new bridge although, the *Echo* commented sourly, the castle's decorations weren't up to much. Lord Bute had done more for his son's 21st birthday a couple of years earlier.

A memorable milestone, then, in Cardiff's maritime history, this link with the docks. But years later Clarence Bridge's only claim to fame would be as finishing point for the great Taff Swim, the race down the river starting at Cardiff (or Canton to the locals) Bridge. Only the oldest inhabitants remembered vaguely why it was called Clarence Bridge – it still is, although it was replaced – and today's youngsters haven't a clue. And nobody really knows now why a nearby pub was called the Avondale, another reminder of the day Jack the – sorry, Prince Eddie, Duke of Clarence and Avondale came to Cardiff.

But that visit looks, in retrospect, like no more than a rehearsal for the day when the King himself rolled up. And not just to open a bridge. No, this was as auspicious a day in the history of the city as the opening of the first Bute dock in 1839 had been. This was the day when the King came to open what would be the last of the great docks.

I Name This Dock
After My Missus

OH YES, Cardiff was truly coming of age. In October, 1905 the town on the banks of the Taff became a city: the news had come in a telegram to the corporation informing them that 'It is His Majesty's pleasure that the borough of Cardiff be constituted a City and that the Chief Magistrate thereof be styled Lord Mayor.' Naturally that meant a public holiday when the aldermen and

In 1907 King Edward VII comes to Cardiff to open the Queen Alexandra Dock, named after his wife. Here the royal yacht enters the dock.

To be welcomed by, among others, Tatem's Torrington packed with 'waifs and strays'. The banner on the side greets the King, Queen and Princess.

Cardiff becomes a city and here is the first City Council meeting in October 1905. 'We did it,' claim the Docksmen.

councillors met in the Town Hall, from then on the City Hall. 'The council chamber,' Our Correspondent reported, 'was crowded. Lord Bute attended, and so did many prominent Docksmen.'

So there we are – no doubt about it, those 'prominent Docksmen' really believed that their efforts had made Cardiff worthy of becoming a city. The jubilation was summed up by the *Echo's* ever-euphoric Man About Town: 'Now it's not Mr or plain Mrs or Miss. It's Good Morning Citizen.

A painting of the scene after docking with the royal party on their dais.

The whole of the town centre was the same – here is Queen Street.

Madame Clara Novello Davies was there with 14-year-old Ivor. Here she is in later life with husband and prodigal son.

Or Fair Morrow Citiziness.' The only question is why Man About Town didn't promote himself to, well, to Man About City. But of course, he'd be there on the milestone day to come.

And that was on 13 June 1907. Remember, in 1907 the moving film was still a rarely-seen novelty while radio and television were undreamed of wonders yet to come. Some citizens might have seen flickering shadows showing the state funeral of the Old Queen on some primitive screen, perhaps even her Golden Jubilee in 1897, for the first films were seen in town at the Empire Theatre in 1896. That year also brought the first news film made in Britain, showing the visit of the Prince and Princess of Wales to Cardiff. But Victoria had been as remote to the people of Tiger Bay and to the Docksmen who employed them as, say, Zeus had been to a citizen of Sparta. And as revered.

Now here came her son, just as godlike a figure, King Edward VII, Emperor of India, Defender of the Faith, Tum-Tum to his friends, for the first visit by a monarch in 250 years. But his picture had been seen in the public prints, so he was less of, well if you like, less of a mystery than his mother. Teddy, they called him, the Uncle of Europe, and here he was, bearded and beaming in Cardiff.

On the day before the royal visit the *Echo* printed columns of information about the King's life – always referring to him as Edward the Peacemaker or the First Gentleman of Europe. The paper was impressed by the preparations. 'If they lasted a week,' observed our old and trusted informant Man About Town, 'I verily believe that every worker would be given a week's holiday with two week's pay and that the schools would be closed for another three months.' So they came out to welcome this greatest of all the great Bute docks, this newest wonder of the maritime world, knowing that it was essential if Cardiff wanted to stop most of the coal trade going to the booming port of Barry. So they'd started work on it in 1897 and now here it was, the day of the opening and by God what a day they would make of it, these Docksmen who really regarded it all as their own personal triumph.

And why not? They could see no end to the torrents of coal flowing down from the valleys, optimists all, every manjack of 'em as they waited for the Arrival. So did thousands of others, crowds behind gaily-decorated barricades praying for the rain to stay away (another flaming June?)

They turned out to see the Queen who had given her name to their new docks – but this picture shows only the King on the right of the carriage.

as they lined up hours before the ceremonies were due to start. To entertain them they had the band of the Grenadier Guards and the famous Madame Clara Novello Davies (14-year-old Ivor doubtless

But here she is, Queen Alexandra, remembered forever in Cardiff because of that dock.

somewhere in the crowd) who was there with her renowned Royal Welsh Ladies Choir. She was wearing, as she always did, the diamond brooch presented to her by Victoria years before after a personal Command Performance. That was when she was given the privilege of calling her choir the Royal Ladies.

At 10 o'clock the Cardiff Railway Company's luxurious saloon steamed up and out stepped Lord Bute and his party. Cheers from the multitude, the omnipresent Man About Town informed his readers as the Noble Lord emerged, the city's own God followed by the demi-gods, Lord Ninian-Stuart, Lord Plymouth, Lord Edmund Talbot and Viscount Tredegar. And then, and over the years you can sense the excitement swell as the hooter sounds, here she comes, the royal yacht, the famous *Victoria and Albert*. On the bridge the King himself, his Queen and

Then, to the strains of *Rule Britannia*, the *Victoria and Albert* sliced through a scarlet ribbon and entered the dock. So, soon afterwards, did the SS *Lady Lewis*, one of Bill Tatem's boats. It was packed with people but... strangely, not a sound from them. Was this, the crowd wondered, a typical act of *les majeste* from Tatem, the roughest, toughest Docksman of 'em all? As the outraged onlookers muttered, all became clear. The ship turned and a huge banner unfurled. On it was written:

'*We cannot shout, we cannot sing, But we can love our gracious king.*'

Underneath in enormous letters: GOD BLESS THE KING AND QUEEN.

Aaaahhhh, sighed the suddenly won-over crowd. There's lovely. For these were the deaf and dumb children of Cardiff and Treforest and the orphans from Nazareth House and the St Margaret's Home of Mercy. Wily old Tatem had stolen the show, but the Queen might not have noticed, as she was deaf as well. More than 60 years after it happened, a Mrs Evans recalled that day in a letter to the *Echo*.

'*I remember (though hazily) all the schoolchildren going out in little boats to meet Queen Alexandra at the opening of the dock named after her. We all had dresses made of butter muslin at sixpence a yard, white Spanish cord daps at sixpence a pair, yards of red, white and blue ribbons as sashes and rosettes in her hair. We thought we were the cat's whiskers.*'

As she said, only hazy memories of that day, but Man About Town set it all down for the record. Thanks to him we know that down on the dockside the King and Queen and daughter Vicky sat on three velvet chairs listening to cheers and receiving bouquets from such favoured youngsters as Master Ronald Forrest, grandson of Sir W.T. Lewis – no doubt to the fury of every watching mother who thought it should have been her little darling. Especially, you think, Madame Clara Novello Davies. Why, her little Ivor, budding

Seen again looking down from her carriage as the King knights Cardiff's Lord Mayor, William Smith Crossman.

The Queen's Dock when Cardiff was one of the world's premier ports.

daughter Victoria, the Princess Royal. And on deck, oompahing away – how did they get there? – the Glamorgan Yeomanry Band. There was even a place for another *Echo* scribe overwhelmed by 'A perfect maze of funnels, masts, streamers and flags. More flags, bunting and Chinese lanterns,' as the ship steamed majestically towards harbour.

And less than half a century after that great day in 1907, empty of shipping, a sad post-war signpost to the future.

musical genius, could have done the job much better…

The First Gentleman of Europe (or Tum-Tum, if you like) sat stolidly through the inevitable speeches, then nodded affably as the great and the good and maybe the not-so-good were presented to him. It was noticeable that Bill Tatem – who else? – didn't back off, head bowed, but turned right round and walked briskly away from his Sovereign. Typical, one veteran Docksman remarked much later, 'he was ignorant, rough and uncouth and could hardly write his name, let alone speak the King's English.' (It didn't stop Tatem getting a title and leaving two million quid in 1942, but we'll come to that later.)

Apparently unfazed by Tatem's about turn, the Monarch rose to his feet, not an easy job when

you've got a 50-inch waist, and made a short speech. 'In the shipping trade of my Kingdom,' he said, 'Cardiff holds an important place.'

None of the shipping tycoons clustered round needed reminding. They were, perhaps, the nearest thing to a collection of oil-rich sheiks these islands have ever known. Like those sheiks they got their wealth out of the ground and the world depended on them. You can imagine their sense of self importance, then, as they climbed into their carriages for the ride into town behind the King and Queen. Out of the dock gates, then down Bute Street where it cost ten golden sovereigns to rent a first floor room looking down over the route – about a month's pay for the girls who usually rented such rooms. The St John Ambulance Brigade got 15 calls in 20 minutes at the corner of

James Street and when the parade reached the end of Bute Street 'a sailor jumped a barrier, in his paroxysm of joy, waving his cap so enthusiastically he got a gracious smile from the Queen.'

Attracting almost as much interest as the monarch when the parade went through Tiger Bay was the horse being ridden by Colonel Doyle, commanding the South Wales Volunteers. The fascinated crowd had been advised by the *Echo* to look out for this 'beautiful chestnut' which had been ridden by the Boer War commander Sir Redvers Bullers during the South African campaign. 'It was shot in the neck outside Ladysmith,' Man About Town revealed, 'but Sir Redvers rode it when the siege was lifted.' You can imagine urchins gazing in awe at this equine hero, asking each other, 'Can you see where it was wounded… can you see the bullet 'ole?'

It was a busy day for Man About Town. So great was the enthusiasm, he found, that at one point as the masses surged forward 'the Volunteers presented their bayonets.' Ladies swooned, one after the other, a certain Miss Hole so overcome she was unconscious for a full half hour, while at one corner a man, 'apparently of the labouring class,' crossed the barrier 'muttering that he had something to say to the King.' He was swiftly hurled back over the barrier to cheers from the crowd. At the City Hall, still fresh-minted and gleaming just a year after its opening, 7,000 schoolchildren sang a welcome and within minutes the Lord Mayor, William Smith Crossman, was Sir William Smith Crossman – 'The first Labour knight,' announced the *Echo*.

The King conducted a couple of opening ceremonies, borrowing a knife from Lord Bute for one bit of ribbon-snipping when the golden scissors wouldn't work, then it was back to the Victoria and Albert and off again to London. The *Echo*'s conclusion when it was all over: 'Cardiff has risen to the occasion. All citizens were linked together by the common joy.'

The greatest year of all was still ahead. But before that would come a final farewell for a hero and some of the most divisive months the docks would ever know.

Bring the South Pole
Back to Cardiff

HE WAS the Lord Mayor of Cardiff, a revered Alderman of the city, full of dignity and gravitas; a man whose measured tread echoed down the local corridors of power. But clearly when it came to geography, he was also a link or two short of the full chain of office.

For when presenting Captain Robert Falcon Scott with the city flag before the explorer's voyage to the South Pole, Alderman John Chappell suggested that it should be nailed to this fabled landmark, a fluttering reminder among the

With more well-wishers aboard the Devonia, plus a band to help the send-off.

Captain Scott's ship Terra Nova leaves Cardiff cheered on by crowds aboard the accompanying paddle steamer Ravenswood. (Welsh Industrial Museum)

windswept Antarctic wastes of the mighty coal-producing port at the other end of the world. We can only guess at the austere Scott's reaction – but we certainly know that Cardiff did him proud. And we also know now, of course, that in the end the journey the city celebrated was a failure. The sort of failure, though, for which the adjective 'heroic' might have been coined. Today the words Scott of the Antarctic instantly evoke visions of a peculiarly British form of heroism best symbolised

perhaps, in those high-noon-of-Empire Edwardian times, by the stiff upper lip, the restrained understatement.

'I am just stepping out... I may be some time...'

The Dash for the South Pole.
The "Terra Nova" R.Y.S. leaving Cardiff, June 15th, 1910.

A souvenir card of the day showing Scott and Lieutenant Evans.

The Terra Nova...

...with Evans, Scott on the bridge alongside the Channel Pilot.

The last words of the sick Captain Oates, aware that he was a liability as he left the sanctuary of the expedition's tent to march towards certain death, embodying all the attributes of what the novelists of his day would undoubtedly have called a very gallant English gentleman. Well, books, films, radio and television have made the world familiar with Scott's dream of being first to the South Pole, the Holy Grail for all explorers; they have conveyed the nightmare he felt at finding himself beaten by the better-prepared Roald Amundsen and his Norwegian team. But no one in Cardiff during those buoyant days in June 1910 ever considered failure, for Scott, in a way, was one of ours – almost adopted by the city.

But let us begin, as someone or other once said, at the beginning...

It might have been an all-Welsh expedition – as Lt Edward Evans (he would end his days as

Admiral Lord Mountevans), some of whose family came from Cardiff was anxious to lead an expedition to the Pole himself. The Editor of the *Western Mail*, one of the most powerful men in the country, gave his backing – 'It ought to be possible to make it a Welsh expedition' – and no one in the city was in any doubt that such a glorious project would dramatically enhance Cardiff's image around the globe. Eventually Scott agreed to co-operate with Evans who would be his second-in-command and the Docksmen of the city, with Daniel Radcliffe at their head, swiftly identified themselves with the mission.

Because of them, Cardiff was to the forefront when it came to raising cash to finance the expedition, the city swiftly contributing £1,400 of the £50,000 needed. The *Western Mail* reported that Captain Scott was so impressed by the city's support that instead of having that legendary Welsh steam coal sent to London by train, he would send the *Terra Nova* herself to collect it at Cardiff. That would be a real showing of the flag, while also showing the city what it was paying for. The Lord Mayor, Docksmen and civic leaders planned to meet the ship as it steamed in on Friday, 10 June, but the *Terra Nova* slipped into the Cardiff Roads 15 hours earlier. Someone telephoned the Lord Mayor (on Cardiff One, perhaps?) so he, Dan Radcliffe and the rest had to rush out to the *Terra Nova* aboard a tug boat to welcome Scott before returning to prepare for the planned wider welcome.

The following morning they went out again, this time aboard a tug owned by Edmund Handcock, a man we will soon meet in a very different role – target for The Most Dangerous Man in Europe.

A rainswept morning but never mind, thousands of citizens lined the shores to cheer the crew into the Roath Dock, banners bravely defying the drizzle. After loading 100 tons of free coal from local collieries to add to the 300 tons already aboard, the men were given weekend

Shipowner Dan Radcliffe, prime fund-raiser who helped finance Scott's voyage and hosted the dinner in Cardiff's Royal Hotel.

leave, the Lord Mayor telling them, 'We want you to have a rare good time,' leaving it for others to warn them of the terrors of Tiger Bay. Instead they were whisked into town, stalwart heroes every one of 'em, the astronauts of their time, going off to unknown, perilous places, and you can bet that they didn't have to buy a drink. And also bet that the drink flowed – Petty Officer Edgar Evans, from Swansea, had to be carried back to the ship. But it's a measure of the feeling the men inspired that when spotted in the Palace Theatre the audience spontaneously sang 'For they are jolly good fellows.'

On Monday, 13 June, Scott and his officers were guests of honour at a splendid farewell dinner in the Royal Hotel – still commemorated each year on the anniversary though the meal

costs more than the 7s 6d per head it did on that long gone night – and at the end of it the Lord Mayor handed over the flag, with that famous instruction to nail it to the South Pole.

He wasn't the only one whose idea of the Pole had apparently been gleaned from halfpenny comic papers like *Chips* – where it was always shown, sometimes striped like a barber's sign, sticking up out of the snow, surrounded, with a casual disregard of wildlife habitats, by polar bears and penguins. A coal-owner took one of the crew members to one side and muttered that it would be worth his while if he could smuggle a couple of splinters of the Pole back – what an enviable souvenir to have on show in his Docks office. While a reporter was even more ambitious, suggesting that the entire Pole should be brought back and installed like a Christmas tree outside the City Hall.

The enthusiasm was so great that the assembled guests, led by the ship-owner Dan Radcliffe, raised another £1,000 on the spot, making it a total of £2,500 from Cardiff. An overwhelmed Captain Scott pledged there and then that when his ship sailed south the Cardiff City arms would fly from his mizzen mast 'in tribute and gratitude'.

Two days later the *Terra Nova* departed with what seemed like the whole of South Wales there to see her off, their cheers scattering the seagulls from the dockside cranes when they saw the Red Dragon flag, specially made by Howells department store, fluttering above the White Ensign. The cheers were even louder when the crew sent up two leeks to hang alongside the flags – would they be raised at the Pole along with that Red Dragon, the crowd must have wondered. The *Terra Nova* with the Lord Mayor and Docksmen aboard was followed by dozens of small boats, with aldermen and councillors packed on to the paddle steamer *Devonia*.

Captain Scott returned to the dockside with the Lord Mayor's party as he was to join the crew later: but they were already planning the great

The plaque in that hotel's 'Captain Scott Room' commemorating the dinner. For years a celebratory banquet with the same menu was held on each anniversary.

The 'Captain Scott' lighthouse in Cardiff's Roath Park. 'How did they get the Terra Nova out of here?'

welcome home he'd be given when he returned – perhaps, hoped our reporter, with the Pole to go up outside City Hall.

And again, as so often happens when you travel back in time to a day when the faded old newspaper in front of you was new, hot from those old-fashioned presses, again you share the feeling of numbness, of disbelief, that must have overcome the city when, almost two years later, the *South Wales Echo* brought the grim ending to the story that had begun with such hope.

You can see them even now, staring silently down at the paper dated 11 February 1913. And how subdued must have been the atmosphere in the Exchange Building and in the dockers' pubs and the Docksmen's clubs on that melancholy day. A search party had stumbled across a tiny tent in the Antarctic. Inside it, three bodies: Scott, Lt H.R. Bowers, and Dr E.A. Wilson. They had reached the Pole on 17 January 1912, only to find the Norwegian flag flying, shattering, heartbreaking proof that Amundsen had beaten them. Petty officer Edgar Evans, the Swansea man who had been entrusted with the city flag by Scott, had died on the way back to that tent; the others some time in March. Now, almost a year later Cardiff learned of the tragedy. A painting of the *Terra Nova* hanging in the Exchange building was draped in black, a service of remembrance was held in St John's Church. The *Terra Nova* returned to Cardiff in June 1913, and 60,000

people were there to welcome her, more sombre, of course, and more subdued than had been the crowds cheering her on her way just three years before.

Today the room where Dan Radcliffe, his brother-in-law Bill Tatem and the other Docksmen assembled is still there in the newly-renovated Royal Hotel, a shrine to those lost heroes. While in the city's Roath Park stands a lighthouse-type clock tower, commemorating those great days of 1910. And yes, there really have been people as naive as that Lord Mayor who wanted the city flag to flutter from the Pole, people who have wondered how Captain Scott managed to get the *Terra Nova* out of the lake and down to the distant docks.

In recent years there have been attacks on Scott, condemnations of his conduct made. But he and his men will always have a place in Cardiff's heart: the city has never forgotten its adopted sons.

Meet 'The Most Dangerous Man in Europe'

WELL, while Scott and his men trekked through the white wilderness things were happening in Cardiff, and those ship-owners who had celebrated so joyously in 1910 found themselves with little to be joyous about in 1911. For they were facing their first great challenge since the strike of 1890. They were up against the immortal Cap'n Tupper.

Years later the newspaper owner Lord Thompson would speak of commercial television as 'a licence to print money.' You can sense the shades of those old time Cardiff magnates scoffing at this revelation. And why not, for they'd discovered their own printing presses half a century before in the shape of shipping and coal: why, they could hardly count the cash flowing in. During that year there were 350 vessels based in Cardiff and to give you an idea of what that meant – well, they made up one-fourteenth of all tramp shipping in the United Kingdom. And as each ship earned an average profit of £10,000, the owners, men like Tatem and Radcliffe, could look those 'Robber Barons' of America, giants like the Carnegies and Rockefellers across the pond, straight in the eye.

More than that: the year before, repair work was carried out on more than a thousand ships in the city's 12 dry docks. So with that kind of money around the men who did the work could scarcely be blamed for wanting a somewhat larger slice of the cake. But the Cardiff owners, obdurate as ever, rejected demands for a national concil-iation board, a uniform scale of wages and control of hiring procedures that hadn't advanced much since Ben Tillett's condemnation of them in 1890.

So the South Wales dockers struck while their national leaders were negotiating with the Port of London authorities. Enter the eccentric described by the acid-tongued F.E. Smith, future Lord Birkenhead, as 'The most dangerous man in Europe, who wants to drench his country in blood from John o'Groats to Land's End.'

Enter Edward Tupper…

They called him Cap'n, although where the title came from no one quite knew. But we are left in little doubt about one thing: Cap'n Tupper was one of the great characters of his time, a strike leader to fill his followers with fire, who took on the Docksmen on his terms, who stepped straight into local folklore during the great docks strike of 1911.

Cheered on by his flat-capped followers, he wore a morning coat and silk topper to union meetings in Bute Street. If such an outfit was good enough for the bosses, he roared, it was good enough for him. After each meeting he'd consume reservoirs of Bass ale – a couple of gallons at a time, some said, and, when topped up, he'd challenge any of the Docksmen to fight him in long-gone Neptune Park, a novel way of settling industrial disputes. Can you imagine Scargill and Macgregor…?

Anyway, the tugboat-owner Edmund Handcock offended Cap'n Tupper more than most by breaking the strictest unwritten rule of all – he employed Chinese labour. So out went the challenge after yet another session with the Bass ale: 'I'll fight you for fifty quid.'

Mr Handcock, perhaps wisely in view of the Capn's reputation, didn't respond. So Tupper marched his men down to Handcock's office, where he repeated his challenge from the road

Captain Tupper giving one of the 14 speeches the Echo claimed he delivered each day to enthusiastic strikers beneath his balcony. The inset shows a close-up of 'the most dangerous man in Europe'.

And here he is in a hansom cab with Herbert Read, the Echo *chief who persuaded him to allow rolls of newsprint through his lines. They lead a parade of wagons laden with paper through the dock gates.*

outside. Again, no response, so the men started throwing chunks of coal (no shortage in 1911) through the office windows. When even that failed to bring out Handcock they set fire to the building and when the firemen arrived they cut their hoses.

This was too much even for police wary of turning Cap'n Tupper into a martyr. He ended up in court facing 16 charges and was remanded on bail although you get the feeling the Docksmen would have settled for a a quick public hanging. But Tupper's dockers, determined to release their paladin from durance vile, armed themselves with a choice assortment of weapons – including frightening coshes made from tarred rope with nails bound into the end, to go with the usual crowbars and hammers. Then they marched raucously down Bute Street and through the city centre, threatening to level the City Hall unless their champion was released.

They were faced by a hastily-assembled police blockade and there hadn't been such a battle outside the castle since Owain Glyndwr came to town. But finally the strikers gave up on the City Hall and wandered back to the docks. On their way they looted barrels of spirits and stout from warehouses which were then burned, embarking on a monumental binge that ended only when a lorry was pushed into the dock.

Clearly hoping to cool things down the authorities released Tupper on bail and this turned out to be a decision bringing one of the most unsavoury chapters in Cardiff's history. For once free, Tupper, a ferociously-fiery orator who could have inspired a convent full of nuns into stoning their stained-glass windows, immediately inflamed his followers by using the age-old tactic of the demagogue – he put the blame for the dockers' ills on foreigners, specifically the Chinese.

'Chinese crews on British ships,' he trumpeted, 'will inevitably bring Chinese dockers to South Wales.'

Tupper wasn't the first to raise the spectre of job-stealing Chinese. In 1908 a local official of the National Seamen's and Firemen's Union claimed that 'as the dumping ground of foreigners Cardiff is known as the scrap heap of Europe. And instead of the Union Jack, the officers of the Shipping Federation ought to fly the Chinese flag.' There was talk of 'hordes' of Chinese being imported while lurid tales spread through the town of opium dens and and that old standby, White Slavery. The *South Wales Daily News* reported that Tupper's men raided Chinese boarding houses to 'rescue' innocent young maidens held in captivity by villains who had fed them drugged

Herbert Read in his editorial sanctum. He was also aboard the Terra Nova *for a spell when it sailed out of Cardiff.*

A different strike, a different era. Dry dock workers see their jobs go after refusing to return to work in 1967 in defiance of union orders.

sweets. No young maidens emerged although the report brought fresh attacks on the 22 Chinese laundries in the city. Hysteria, then: but the year before Tupper's call to arms only two per cent of men signing on ships in Cardiff were Chinese.

No matter! This was the Yellow Peril, predicted for so long in those lurid weekly 'Penny Dreadfuls', come to life. This meant hordes of Asiatics in Cardiff to take the dockers' jobs. It didn't take long for rumours to spread that already more Chinese strike-breakers were being imported and this enraged the dockers even more. Inoffensive Chinese laundreymen saw their premises attacked again, shops and lodging houses were stoned and looted, racism was rampant.

That was when F.E. Smith delivered his famous judgment: 'Tupper was the most dangerous man in Europe...' But the *Echo* seemed entranced by the anarchic Cap'n. Reporters were assigned to follow him around the town and told to clock up the number of harangues delivered in a single morning.

'FOURTEEN SPEECHES IN A DAY' the headline shouted, and every one an incitement. Yet the paper was sympathetic to the strikers whose jobs, it felt, really were in danger of being

taken by the Chinese seamen. Herbert Read, chief of the editorial staff and a power in the land, pleaded with Tupper to allow rolls of newsprint to be unloaded at the docks for the *Echo's* presses.

'We will back the strikers,' he said. 'But without newsprint it will be impossible.'

George V was crowned halfway through the strike but there was no pause for celebration. Night after night the *Echo* carried stories of assaults on coloured seamen and those Chinese accused of job-stealing. A typical paragraph: 'Two men were fined for attacking a hapless Chinaman and causing damage to his trousers to the extent of 7s 6d.' Tell us more, you beg. Damaged trousers? So what did they *do*? you ask. But that brief paragraph was the lot.

But the paper consistently appealed for reason and, unusually for the times, refused to blame the strikers for the violence, especially after a battalion of the Lancashire Fusiliers was brought in to reinforce the police. Memories of the Tonypandy riots the year before were still vivid, and thoughts of soldiers marching once more into South Wales to put down the local population brought even more sympathy for the strikers.

'The lesson,' the *Echo* warned, 'is not to let the police or the military break heads indiscriminately... not to use the butt end of a gun, the point of a bayonet or a constable's stave.' Tupper also condemned the violence even though he'd encouraged much of it, for he saw that frustration in Cardiff was growing and that things could truly get right out of hand. Cardiff dockers earned a lot less than those in Newport and Swansea, and felt exploited by their bosses. And when they learned that even more Chinese were being hired by these bosses to work British ships, a city-threatening confrontation looked on the cards. But the strike eventually ended and the preparations for war – predicted mainly by sensational novelists since the latter day Teutonic knight Kaiser Wilhemn had come to power – brought an end to the fears of unemployment.

Senghenydd:
The True Cost of Coal

BUT before the first shots of 1914 were fired Cardiff would see the great bonanza year of 1913 when the docks reached their glorious peak. It was also the year when we would discover the true cost of coal as the most appalling disaster of all struck South Wales.

1913... Historians tell us it was the last year of a Golden Age, a year enshrined forever in the hearts of those who lived through it as the century's true watershed, the end of a glittering era, in retrospect, the end of innocence. But for the coal and shipping barons of South Wales it was the year when their golden goose was at its fattest, when even the awesome amounts of fine Welsh steam coal being mined could scarcely keep up with the demand. It was the year, old timers used to recall, when ships lined up in the Channel, waiting their turns to enter the docks as the never-ending torrent cascaded down from the valleys. It was said that you could cross the entire dock area simply by stepping from ship to ship. Percy Davies, an old timer who actually lived inside the docks, had a more colourful term – 'A monkey could swing across from yard arm to yard arm.' We'll meet Percy later as he pickets his own home!

1913: the year the Docksmen turned their Exchange Building into King Coal's Counting House. Awed Cardiffians told each other that when standing on the Floor (always sanctified by that capital F) of the Exchange you could stretch your hand out in any direction, and anyone you touched would be a millionaire. An exaggeration? Perhaps. But that year over ten million tons of coal went out of Cardiff packed into some 8,000 ships by around 2,000 trimmers. They shipped out even more from Barry – world champ for this

King Coal's Counting House – the Coal and Shipping Exchange, the heart of the docks in the glory years. Cully's famous restaurant where the tycoons gathered makes sure no one misses the sign.

Ready for work in the Exchange across the road – down to the bowler hats...

Before World War One...

...and in the 1920s.

never-to-be-forgotten period – and altogether in a record-shattering 12 months they ripped some 57 million tons out of the Welsh coalfields.

Seven years earlier Lloyd George, the greatest Welsh statesman of his time, perhaps of any time, had addressed the Cardiff Docksmen. His message had been: 'Don't put all your trust in coal.' How they laughed, those men with unshakeable faith in the future. The Welsh Wizard, observed one Docksman, Sir William Gunn (although it's a safe bet he didn't describe him like that) 'should keep his wisdom for the slate quarries of North Wales.'

Already the big men of shipping and coal were building their monolithic office blocks, monuments to their own egos, perhaps, but dramatic symbols of boundless faith in the future. And why not? When Lord Bute (God rest his soul, they might have muttered), had built that first fine dock only about 10,000 people lived in Cardiff. In this year of grace, 1913, there were almost 200,000. And who could doubt (you can hear those Docksmen muttering again), who can doubt that we have helped make the city what it is. So they gathered in the Exchange, their temple to Moloch on Mount Stuart Square, a bunch of

The legendary Floor offering only a glimpse of great days gone, when it was packed.

bucanneering brothers who'd each collected a winning ticket in life's lottery, who made fortunes in a single morning, who were, to borrow a phrase that would come much, much later, Masters of the Universe.

But while the Docksmen counted their cash, the people of the valleys counted the cost. For 1913, that year of dizzying profits, was also the year of the greatest calamity in Welsh mining history. On 14 October, 440 men and boys died in an explosion in Senghenydd Pit, the heart was ripped out a community, a village died. On one street alone they counted 40 dead. That was Commercial Street. The people of High Street mourned 33.

And in the 1950s, the captains and the coal kings gone forever, an empty Floor.

The imposing entrance now opening on to exhibitions and concerts but still suggesting the optimism of those Docksmen who believed coal would last forever.

But the lions still keep guard above the clocks which seem stuck forever at Low Tide.

Soon after eight o'clock that morning a miner's lamp went out. Dai Davies, master haulier, took it to be relit at the lamp station. By one of those awesome flicks of fate which have so often changed history, at the very moment Dai held out his lamp the roof collapsed 200 yards away. A jet

Less impressive but still a money-maker – the offices of the Cyfartha Company on West Canal Wharf, Mr Watkins Lewis master of all he surveys standing outside.

of explosive gas escaped, rushing into the station where Dai's lamp was being lit. Naked flame plus gas equalled – inferno. Senghenydd's agony had begun.

Fathers and sons lay together in death. One of the nurses tending the bodies came across her own son. He was 14. He had started work that day. The valley just 20 miles from Cardiff's docks was left with 205 widows, 542 fatherless children and 62 old, dependent parents.

Down on those docks, in the little streets all round, in Tiger Bay, in those places where men had been, as we said, almost umbilically linked to those other men who produced the coal on which their livelihoods too, depended, in those places they felt a comradeship – dockers and seamen helping swell the fund being raised to aid those widows, those fatherless kids. Take any mining village of the time and you knew it was dependent on the docks – whether Cardiff, Port Talbot, Barry or Newport. And in turn the dockers, the

They knew the cost of coal in the Exchange: they counted the cost in Senghennyd where 440 died in a pit explosion in 1913, the greatest year in the history of the docks. The victims go on their last journey between ranks of mourners.

trimmers, the labourers, and yes, the Docksmen themselves, were dependent on those miners.

And that is why it's necessary to say something about Senghenydd, which stands as a symbol for

A sombre crowd waits at the pit top for news of survivors.

But the coffins are readied as the dead are recovered.

Far from the Exchange a woman holds her baby, hoping against hope that her husband will be coming home. He never will.

every other mining disaster, which is the bleak ticket showing the true price of the coal on which the fortunes of Cardiff's docks were founded. Yet we were on the brink of a greater cataclysm than any mine explosion. We were heading for a war

which would ultimately mean richer pickings than ever for the Docksmen – before seeing fortunes melt away like that fabled fairy gold in the space of a single year.

The City of Dreadful Knights

IT WOULD all be over by Christmas.

That was the mantra recited by all but the most diehard pessimist when Britain went to war on 4 August 1914. The *South Wales Echo* front page thundered out its message in huge type: YOUR KING AND COUNTRY NEED YOU.' While the *Western Mail's* lead editorial said: 'Let it not be recorded to our eternal shame that young men were playing cricket and football while the nation's call for soldiers continued unfulfilled.' No danger of that: so great was the response that emergency recruiting stations had to be set up. There was something approaching euphoria as Cardiff's young men flocked to the colours and

It's 1914 and war is on the way. But this display shows there's no shortage of foods in Cardiff's docks. This window won a prize for Reese and Gwillim, grocers of James Street.

why not, after all, it would all be over by Christmas.

And is it being cynical to wonder whether the 40 young men from James Howells shop who signed up together didn't, perhaps, think that the army might be more fun and offer more romance than life behind a counter? After all, it was only for a few months: it would all be over by Christmas. Meanwhile sandwich board men marched through the docks with the message, 'You cowards, you shirkers...' and the entreaty to come and fight. Oswald Sturdy, a teacher from a Tiger Bay school, took them up on it and went straight to Maindy Barracks. He became part of the famous Cardiff Pals, the battalion made up of local lads from every strata of class and sphere of employment, many of them office workers from the docks. Our Mr Sturdy, incidentally, would later find the company cook washing his feet in the tub from which he'd just dispensed the stew – preparing to make the tea in it once his ablutions were finished.

Yes, men – and boys – from the docks would rush to sign up. But the docks themselves would play a vital part in winning this war. Why, didn't everyone know that the British Navy, those mighty dreadnoughts, that great grey fleet, didn't every one know that they ruled the waves and would hammer the Hun? Of course, and the lifeblood of this vast fleet was the coal tumbling down from the valleys, shipped out of Cardiff's docks, the fine steam coal which powered the vessels we still called Men o' War.

Cardiff did its bit on the very first day of war when four German ships tied up in the docks were taken over, but during the years that followed we found it wasn't the surface ships but the dreaded submarine, the U-Boat, which would do most damage. As the war went on – as Christmas after

David Lloyd George, the war leader who warned Cardiff's Docksmen, 'Put not all your trust in coal.' Go back to the slate quarries, they told him. But he was right.

Christmas came and went and as the young clerks from the docks died one after another – the U-Boat threat became ever more potent. So many vessels were sunk that practically all Cardiff's shipping was commandeered, tycoons like John Cory and Dan Radcliffe becoming accustomed to the news that yet another of their old favourites had gone to the bottom. Bill Tatem's company lost nine vessels but the Docksmen were compensated for every ship lost – and Tatem got an extra bonus when, on 28 June 1918, he became The Baron Glanely of St Fagans in recognition of his contribution to the war effort. Still, the Prince of Wales came to Cardiff to lend some – moral support?

There wasn't much, though, for the families of the crews who went down with the ships. Just plenty of mourning in Tiger Bay and in the little streets spreading off from James Street, although the sea, whether men were at war or not, had always been the enemy. In that May before war broke out five pilots died when their cutter collided with another vessel in the Bristol Channel.

The city earned even more fame when the cruiser HMS *Cardiff*, launched in 1917, led the surrendered German fleet into Scapa Flow. The memory of that day is trapped triumphantly forever on a huge painting now hanging in the City Hall. What a symbol of the city's place in the

The Prince of Wales visits the wartime docks.

world of shipping, those Docksmen might have thought. For here they were, at war's end, looking forward to greater times and bigger profits than ever before. They'd already seen their fortunes grow beyond belief, but that seemed no more than the start for them as they sat in their fine houses far away from Loudoun Square which had once been *the* address.

In 1919 more than 100 new shipping companies worth £10 million were registered and in 1920 another 60 worth £71 million, reflecting the way in which shipping was at its highest-ever premium, in frighteningly short supply as so much had been lost to the U-Boats. The following year some 400 vessels were registered in Cardiff with 122 companies doing business. So it seemed like a

good investment when Edgar Edwards of Llandaff almost casually paid £1,800,000 for Sir Walter Runciman's fleet. So great was the demand that when a potential buyer approached Sir Herbert Cory he was told that yes, he could have the Cory ships – if he paid the price. That price was eight and a quarter million, a colossal sum in those post-war years, beyond comprehension to the coalminers and coal trimmers of the land.

Those were the days when one man bought 50,000 tons of coal one morning in one corner of the Exchange, walked across the Floor, and sold it at a shilling a ton profit – without ever seeing the coal or laying out a penny. Not bad: £2,500 profit for a couple of minutes' work. Around 20 years pay for one of the trimmers. These men handled

The Prince of Wales on tour.

deals like this without flinching, yet they knew the value of every pound. One ship owner with £600,000 in a deposit account quarrelled with his bank manager over a penny interest and estimates of millionaires living in Cardiff varied wildly – some said 26, others only half a dozen. But there were enough of them to earn titles, bringing Cardiff the label The City of Dreadful Knights.

Who now remembered Lloyd George's warning – put not your trust (or all of it, anyway) in coal? Why, men like Bill Tatem, spending like looney lottery winners, would claim that there was no end to the torrents of black gold, no end to the world's need for it.

Then came the 1920 strike in the Welsh coalfields. Soon stocks of coal were exhausted,

American interests snapped up customers, and exports for the first time from Poland coupled with the cheap coal production in France helped nail down the coffin lid.

Who would have dreamed only a year before that the city would see Docksmen selling off their ships at ludicrous prices, not panic-buying but panic-selling? One speculator who paid £600,000 for four ships in 1919 – another licence to make money – was forced to sell them for £100,000 the lot. Another ship that cost £100,000 went for half that price within two years. The case of just one Docksman offers dramatic testimony to the decline. In 1919, J.C. Gould formed his own company – Gould Steamships and Industrials Ltd – with a capital of

HMS Cardiff, *the 'city's own ship' which led the surrendered German fleet into Scapa Flow.*

£3 million. In that first year he showed a profit of £500,000. Yes, you have to repeat it: this was a licence to print money. Gould bought a grand mansion in St Mellons and a flat in Park Lane, London's Millionaires' Row – and just six years after he set up his business, six years after he had looked forward to ever-growing profits, he was bankrupt. And died penniless.

The Docksmen could look back to 1919 as a year when everything went their way. We see it now, perhaps, as the High Noon of Cardiff as coal port. But it brings back other, bitter memories. For it was also the year when race war came to the ports of South Wales, bringing death to the streets of the city.

Bigotry and Battles in the Bay

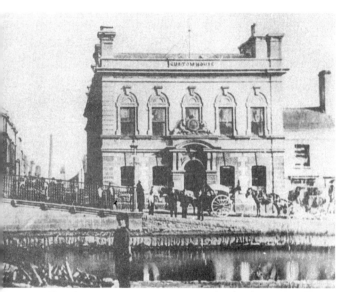

The Custom House on East Canal Wharf. One small boy peers at the photographer, unaware that in a few years this will be a battleground.

WHEN it was all over a stunned South Wales stood back to count the cost. It was heavy. Three men dead, scores seriously wounded, houses gutted by fire, shops and restaurants smashed. And Cardiff's reputation as a place of racial tolerance forever tarnished – there had been riots before, though never on this scale. They had been between seamen of different races battling over jobs, the colour of money rather than skin the reason. As far back as 1879 Greek seamen, regarded in Cardiff as the first 'scabs', had marched through the streets of Tiger Bay and the docks bellowing 'Send out your blacks and we'll murder every one of them.'

Now, in 1919 we would see far more violence in Cardiff and in the adjoining ports of Newport and Barry. Years before the phrase 'Long, hot summer' echoed round the globe as black fought

And here it is in 1910, showing exactly where the battle lines would be drawn in 1919, just below the bridge between the York Hotel to the left of the bridge and the Glendower behind it.

The Custom House, now the headquarters of the Welsh Rugby Union.

The Golden Cross, opposite the entrance to Bute Street, 'where innocence dropped'.

white in America, as great cities blazed, long before this, South Wales had a short hot summer of its own. Rampaging mobs in Newport, gun battles in Cardiff, home-made spears, razors and knives flashing in Barry.

At the bottom of it all – fear. Fear for jobs. Fear for housing. Fear of 'mongrelisation'.

The 'War to end Wars' was over and as the summer of 1919 approached the servicemen were returning. Not to that promised land fit for heroes but to a drastic shortage of housing and a daunting lack of work. In Cardiff there were 2,000 registered unemployed and most of them were ex-servicemen suddenly thrust back into civvy street.

There were also more than 1,000 unemployed coloured seamen, displaced by white sailors returning from the Royal Navy and auxiliary services. The same trend was clearly evident in

other ports. In June 1919, South Wales was an explosion waiting to happen.

To illustrate the attitude of the Cardiff 'establishment' towards its black and brown citizens, those people who lived mainly in Tiger Bay, just

Where we met the Man from Georgia. Leonard Davies, manager, seen in 1979 as plans are made to demolish the old building the following year.

listen to the words of one man that summer, a man named David Williams: 'I am against black men playing cricket in Cardiff as white flannels are more revealing than corduroys, and make black men more attractive to white girls.' He added that he disapproved of young girls 'being allowed to admire such beasts.' The words of a ranting, sexually-repressed racist? Well yes. But this bigot also happened to be the Cardiff Chief Constable. No surprise, then, that his report when the riots ended was a prejudiced piece of self justification.

This, then, was the climate in the docks and Tiger Bay when to be black or brown or yellow was to be made to feel inferior. But the war had changed a lot of things: about 1,000 coloured men sailing out of South Wales ports had died and the old ways were changing. And so, in Newport on 6 June, when a white woman claimed that she had been insulted by a coloured man it was seen by whites as a challenge to the established order. Early *Echo* reports spoke of fighting, with mobs storming houses occupied by coloured men. The paper couldn't have dreamed of what was coming next, and neither could those 'respectable' Cardiffians tucked away in their suburbs.

For Newport sent out the signal that there would be no surrender by the coloured population, no equivalent of marching to the back of the bus when told. The besieged householders there used revolvers against their attackers, arming themselves, as well, with pokers and staves. But they were driven out at last by a 3,000-strong mob, their furniture was taken to a nearby railway siding and burned. Among that furniture was a piano, source, you'd guess, of so much joy in happier times, now a symbol of intolerance.

They swept down Newport's Commercial Street smashing windows, looting Chinese laundries, and even Greek lodging houses were attacked as every foreigner became a target. By the end of that first night 20 coloured men and only two whites had been arrested. There were more sporadic outbreaks the next night but this time the police were ready and were able to clear the streets. The *Echo* headline told readers how: BATON CHARGE AT NEWPORT.

One of the white rioters haltingly explained the feeling behind the attacks. 'We went out to France and when we came back we find these foreigners have got our jobs, our businesses and our houses. And we can't get rid of them.'

In Cardiff they read the *Echo* and wondered – can it happen here? The scent of rebellion was in the air and down in Tiger Bay and the docks families prepared for the worst. It looked inevitable. But Cardiff had to wait. The infection spread next to Cadoxton, on the fringe of Barry Dock. On Wednesday, 11 June, a discharged white soldier, Fred Longman, went up to a West Indian fireman and ordered him to 'Go back to your own street.' A scuffle started and other white men joined in. One of them, clearly prepared for trouble-making, hit the fireman, Charles Emmanuel, with a poker. Emmanuel pulled out a knife and stabbed Longman in the heart. That was the first death, inflaming all the prejudices against 'knife-carrying foreigners.' Tradition of the time had it that the white man's weapon was, of course, the chivalrous straight left – forget that Emmanuel was attacked by someone using a poker. Anyway, as Longman fell, Emmanuel and a friend fled with a crowd of howling whites behind them. He was arrested, luckily for him in view of the temper of the mob, and was later sentenced to five years on a charge of manslaughter.

So Cadoxton exploded. White crowds roamed the streets all night, smashing windows, attacking any foreigner they saw. The next day 60 extra police were drafted in to fight back a crowd described as 'white workmen' attacking a chip shop kept by a white woman and her black husband.

Then it was Cardiff's turn.

Albert Allen, an ex-policeman who worked the area at the time, remembered the Cardiff riot starting because coloured men had taken their 'lady friends' (prostitutes, he explained), to Newport for a day out. He belonged to the mounted section of the city police and that evening was detailed to patrol the area around East Canal Wharf, the boundary between Tiger Bay, the docks and the town itself. Given the events in Newport and Cadoxton the authorities expected trouble and this looked like the spark to start the fire.

They knew of the trip to Newport and knew also that there were pimps waiting by the bridge over the canal for the return trip. The old policeman claimed years later that the pimps had been conscripted for war service and that their prostitutes had gone to live with coloured men 'who treated them very well.' So at about nine o'clock that night they were ready when the wagon carrying the girls and their boy friends got back.

The *Echo* report the following day gave the background: 'A brake containing a number of coloured men and white women was going along East Canal Wharf. It attracted a crowd.'

No mention of pimps waiting – but right about attracting a crowd. It seems likely there were hotheads in Cardiff aching to emulate the mobs in Newport and Cadoxton, and here was their chance. Three men were hauled from the brake and badly beaten and as the white crowd grew so reinforcements came up from the Bay to do battle. The fighting began by the York Hotel with anything that came to hand used as weapons. Iron railings torn off fencing by the canal were used until a revolver shot took the police right into the action. The bullet went through a window of the York Hotel and the crowd separated, but then the mob brushed aside the police and raced into Tiger Bay and the docks.

They set a house on fire on Homfray Street then got the news that was like petrol on the flames. A white man, Harold Smart, had died after having his throat slashed with a razor in Caroline Street. That started the smashing up of Arab lodging houses and even the ransacking of houses in Adamsdown, no part of the docks.

The next day trouble spread to the town centre. A British soldier was arrested after a quarrel with a coloured man on the corner of Wood Street and St Mary Street. He broke a window and was arrested but so menacing was the crowd that gathered that the police fled into the Royal Hotel – scene of the Captain Scott dinner almost three years to the day earlier. An officer arguing with the protective crowd was told:' He is one of us and has fought for us, not like the blacks.'

Trouble continued throughout the day – a black man thrown from a tramcar – but the real violence came that night. At about eight o'clock crowds who had gathered on Custom House Street charged down Bute Street and the reason given in next day's *Echo* clearly didn't give the whole story: 'The origin was was a dispute between a woman of the Bute Street walking type and a black man who flashed a razor…'

That was the explanation given. You have to wonder – how did the mob gathered on Custom House Street know this? Clearly they were out for trouble and were so successful in finding it as the most vicious hours of the rioting began that the *Echo's* huge headlines showed something of a shift in ground: FRENZY OF RACE FEUD – BLACK BAITING IN BUTE TOWN.

It was more than 'black baiting'. The mob wrecked boarding houses and cafés and one black man was so badly beaten he died later from a fractured skull. Murder charges against six white men would be dropped for lack of evidence… The rioting spread from Tiger Bay to the docks where the Princess Royal Hotel was attacked. Ironically, one white man was shot through the hand as fire hoses played into rooms on the top floor; but then came the most inflammatory shot of all.

John Donovan, of the town's notorious Mary Ann Street, was a well-known rugby player and runner, a local celebrity with a healthy personal following. You can imagine the reaction when he dropped, a bullet through his heart, while wearing the Mons Star awarded during his four years in France. That made the rampage even worse and on the afternoon of Friday the 13th, a date that lived up to its ominous reputation, frightened coloured men leaving Cardiff with seabags over their shoulders needed police escorts to avoid the ever-growing mobs.

Even outsiders joined in. French soldiers attacked an Algerian while Australian troops beat a Malay who had strayed out of the docks. The violence seemed contagious, an excuse to release all the pent-up feelings of racism shared by so many. By then Loudoun Square, Maria Street,

Angelina Street and Sophia Street had been turned into what amounted to an armed camp with sentries posted, guns at the ready. The fighting continued but the streets were finally cleared when the mounted police were ordered to ride through the street as fast as they could, hitting anyone who got in the way.

All over, then. But stories of individual attacks unreported at the time would emerge in the weeks to come. Among them the sickening story of a white woman married to a coloured man who had been stripped by a crowd including women before having her teeth knocked out. Later in the year, 18 white and ten coloured men appeared in court, their punishments ranging from small fines to 20 months hard labour. Meanwhile about 200 of Cardiff's coloured population were 'repatriated', but in spite of demands from whites, many other coloured men refused to leave. They were British subjects, they insisted. They remained.

Most Cardiffians were distant from the riots, secure in their suburban laagers. But they saw the price that had been paid in the *Echo*: photographs of ruined shops and cafes, burned houses, images of police patrolling the streets. Indeed, so traumatised were readers by events that most

Some of the reasons why the Golden Cross survived to become a listed building. The beautiful tiled murals showing the castle and Cardiff's first real Town Hall on St Mary Street.

agreed with the *Echo*'s demand that the police should be armed. Given the attitude of their chief constable towards 'lesser breeds' it's as well that they weren't.

So the short, hot summer ended. It was a watershed in the city's race relations and things would never be the same again.

Over the years Cardiff seems to have forgotten all this. These days you hear people talk about the way 'we've always been a tolerant city... there is no prejudice.'

I thought that, even though I had played with Bay boys, spent night after night in the old Central Boys Club and ambled along Bute Street for most of my life without thought, never a thought about colour. Until, some time in the early 1950s. I wrote about it years after, in *The Guardian* and the headline was: 'Colour Blind in Tiger Bay.' After the usual burblings about life as a lad the point was hammered home that I had never been aware of any sort of discrimination. I remember writing that even 'the most dismaying of Negro film comedians, those loose-lipped mumblers of 'Yassuhs' and 'JeeEEEhosephats' never caused any embarrassment, even in the old Central Cinema. They accepted Jack Benny's Rochester as a black man in much the same way as we accepted Lou Costello as white: neither was typical, both were caricatures. We could laugh at each.

And as conscription approached a mate could say 'This nigger ain't joining no Navy' and no one worried. At those dances favoured by us all, miniature discos, you'd call 'em now, whose owner had invested in a dozen '78s', black danced with white and no one turned purple. That odd whirring sound, you sensed, was that long gone chief constable (remember him?) spinning in his grave.

Ah yes. I lived an illusion. Until...

Until we found ourselves sitting in the Golden Cross across from Bute Street one Saturday afternoon, half an hour to closing time, sipping, saving the mouth-constricting Brains bitter, watching the clock, fingers crossed, waiting for salvation in the shape of a wallet accompanied by someone in need of company. Hallelujah! It came at twenty to three (closing time three o'clock then, even in the Golden Cross): an American Air Force sergeant. From Georgia. The Golden Cross was clearly not the first pub he'd visited since coming to Cardiff.

He was a long way from home but he was here, by golly, for a good time and you-all, he said, could help him. Move over, he yipped. You're drinking with me. He produced a bottle – maybe Jack Daniels or something equally esoteric – and a crackling wallet and we, as invited, bounced across the bar to greet him. We-all, that is, but one. A lad whose name is now lost to me stayed in his seat. 'Come on,' I cried, having no shame at all in those days of empty pockets, 'come on, it's on him. You heard.'

It was his local. It was his meeting place. Yet the Man from Georgia raised a Deep South spectre and this one among us all was impervious to persuasion. His colour, he guessed, would make him unwelcome at a table presided over by a Man from Georgia. He refused to join the company.

'I got my pride, see,' he said.

And there in the Golden Cross, innocence dropped. I realised that all the time *they* had been playing. *We* had accepted them as mates, and in some gangs we had taken orders from them and we had never, ever seen the difference.

But *they* had.

And maybe, I now reflect, they had been playing a game. They had humoured us, knowing perhaps, that childhood and adolescence would end and that, at some time or other, the world would be bigger for all of us than Tiger Bay or Loudoun Square and that the colour of a skin would matter. And when I wrote that for *The Guardian* I was aware that the black faces of boyhood, each so easily recognisable, had melted into one multi-coloured mass as immigration added more black faces, feared-by-many black faces, a spectre that haunts us still.

Well, I wondered many years after that Saturday afternoon in the Golden Cross, had he been, maybe a bit paranoid? Then I met an old friend, a much-respected man from the Bay. It was at the time when they were rebuilding the Bay, putting up what the locals called Yuppie flats on the other side of Bute Street over the railway line. A classic case of 'the other side of the tracks.'

'There are times,' he said, 'when I feel like a stranger in my own city.'

Because he was black.

That *Guardian* headline, 'Colour Blind in Tiger Bay', spoke of the recent past. Time, now, to go back to a more distant past.

Galloping Gertie
Goes to War

WELL, we've got a General Strike and a Depression coming along, not to mention another World War and before the end we'll be mourning the death of the docks and the end of Tiger Bay. So let's have a little holiday – let's take a trip or two aboard those bouncing little belles of the briny, the paddle steamers.

And why not? For they are as much a part of the docks and the Bay as any of the great ships that steamed their way around the world. The men of Tiger Bay might have sailed off on voyages to exotic parts, trips that took a year or so; their families could step down to the end of the road and take a trip that brought them back in time for tea. They did it on what everyone called 'pleasure boats', and the description was, well, just right.

The first primitive paddle steamers from Somerset flipped their way up the old route of the Taff, passengers disembarking at the bottom of Quay Street. Among them was Benjamin Disraeli, one day to become Queen Victoria's favourite Prime Minister, who came to Cardiff to see a lady

Paddle steamers weren't always geared for pleasure trips. Here are Kate, La Belle Marie *and* Iona, *little vessels used as ferry boats from Cardiff to Penarth.*

friend – you can still find a couple of pubs claiming Dizzy Slept 'Ere. By the 1830s excursions across the Channel or along the coast were commonplace, the most memorable outing of all coming in April 1838 when they paddled out of Cardiff to see Brunel's marvellous *Great Britain* steaming away on her maiden voyage to America, the first ship able to carry enough coal to take her all the way to the New World where buffalo still roamed the Great Plains and Abe Lincoln was an unknown young lawyer.

As the century moved towards the halfway mark, so many outings left the docks that Weston-super-Mare's daily news sheet complained that the town was being 'invaded by trippers'. They got their revenge in 1847 when 250 passengers from Weston stepped ashore in Cardiff's new dock preceded by a blaring brass band. It was music all the way: you could travel to Weston for 2s and that included a concert from a 28-piece band, a corps of drum and fife players and a troupe of 'glee' singers

Passengers from Cardiff were told that 'those who are fond of immersion can be accommodated with bathing machines and attendants,' but anyone who has seen Weston with the tide out will suspect that the Cardiff trippers were probably relieved when the town council banned bathing 'within sight of inhabited houses'. The big breakthrough came in 1887. And we are not talking about the opening of the Roath Dock or the completion of that fairytale fantasy Castel Coch by the third Marquess of Bute. No, this was the year when one of the great names in Cardiff's maritime history embedded itself in the public consciousness.

For this was the year when the first *Waverley* came down from Scotland. It was so successful after being chartered by a group of local businessmen, that her canny Scottish owners decided to operate her themselves. Those owners were called – you guessed it – Messrs P. & A. Campbell. And they would become as legendary a name in Cardiff shipping circles as Tatem or Cory or Radcliffe. In 1891 the *Ravenswood*, the first paddle steamer built exclusively for Bristol Channel trade, made her maiden voyage with 1,200 cheering passengers aboard. She was billed as 'the Greyhound of the Bristol Channel' and was swiftly followed by the *Westward Ho*, the *Cambria* and, most famous of all those early White Funnel ships, the *Britannia*.

During those golden Edwardian years when the sun never stopped shining nor the sea sparkling, Campbell's ran ten steamers and when you look at the old photographs, when you see those straw-boatered lads and their lasses frozen forever in a carefree time long past, well, you can feel the gaiety, the anticipation rising from the page. Thousands upon thousands of men and women and their kids hopped aboard at the Pier Head after travelling through a Tiger Bay that had been till then almost as mythical to them as the Land of Oz. There were rivals: the Barry Railway Company and the Barry and Bristol Channel Steamship Line paddled away as well. They

But this is how we remember them – the Glen Gower *preparing to cast off from Cardiff in 1952 for a Whitsun trip.*

weren't about to let Cardiff collect the cream, for this was a time when Barry was flexing its muscles as its docks prospered mightily. The Barry companies eventually amalgamated to become the Red Funnel Line but in 1911 P. & A. Campbell took over the ships and at the start of what they called the Great War had 13 afloat.

Those little pleasure steamers went off to war, one of them, almost unbelievably, paddling its way around the Dardanelles, almost as big a disaster for Britain then as Dunkirk would be years later. And yes, the pleasure boats would be there as well and some would earn immortality,

After the war Campbell's fought off another challenge, this time from the Yellow Funnel Fleet, but again they were too strong and took over this rival as well, bringing the famous *Brighton Belle* and *Brighton Queen* to Cardiff. So all through the 1920s and 1930s the steamers paddled away from the Pier Head, off to pick up at Penarth Pier perhaps, then across to Weston or Ilfracombe or along the coast to Tenby, and no one aboard the *Brighton Belle* or the *Brighton Queen* or the *Glen*

And here's Iona *passing the Pier Head on her way back to Cardiff.*

And here she is, this time leaving Newport.

Gower, especially the *Glen Gower*, no one could have guessed that before too long these happy little ships would be transformed into lifelines for thousands of shell-shocked soldiers.

So let us now salute them, but especially the *Glen Gower*, owed so much by so many.

They called her Galloping Gertie. And although the name irresistibly brings to mind thoughts of some high-kicking old brassy blonde trouper from Music Hall days, it became remembered and revered forever by almost 3,000 men during Britain's darkest hour.

These were the soldiers who sailed to safety from Dunkirk aboard her, filling decks only a year or two earlier thronged with carefree holiday-makers. For 18 years Gertie had played around the Bristol Channel, frolicking over the waters, bouncing from Cardiff to Minehead and back, loud with the laughter of families out for a breath of the briny. She'd been a fun ship.

But as May slipped into June during that epochal summer of 1940, Gertie was a work ship. She was part of what went affectionately down in history as the 'Welsh Navy', the paddle steamers plucked from giving pleasure to people, then transformed into saving lives. Yes, the paddle steamers that had been part of Cardiff's history were now honoured members of the most astonishing armada ever assembled, those 'little ships' that braved the Dunkirk storm to help make a miracle.

Well, we know she'd been christened the *Glen*

Then the paddle steamers went to war. Here's the Waverley *(not the present one) lying off Dunkirk in June 1940, her decks packed with soldiers being evacuated. A bit different from her pre-war trips from Cardiff to Ilfracombe. She was sunk by German bombers a few months after this picture was taken.*

Gower but she earned her other, more famous name after a record-breaking run of 22 hours from Troon, where she was built, to Bristol. That sea-slapping paddle should have been the high point of her life and it was – until those infinitely more important trips across the English Channel. Odd, for those men and women of South Wales who'd sailed with them to think of their paddle steamers turned into miniature men o'war. But off they went in 1939, all ten Campbell steamers, to serve as minesweepers.

They were perfect for the job as they'd proved in World War One. Their shallow draft plus what sailors said was an ability to turn, reverse and stop on a sixpence (how do you get a sixpence to float?) made them difficult targets. In that 1914-18 conflict the delighted men of the Royal Navy who watched them twisting and turning called them 'butterfly boats'. Shades of Ali with his 'float like a butterfly, sting like a bee.'

Humming birds might have been a better description as they danced and dazzled over the water, but now these birds were playing at being hawks.

A quarter century after it all happened Edward Rees recalled the way it was. He was Galloping Gertie's chief engineer, and while out in the North Sea on a mine-sweeping operation the signal came: 'Return to harbour immediately.' Back to the Tyne to take on coal and extra ammunition

This shows how vulnerable the paddle steamers were as a naval officer waits to be taken off the beaches.

But they'd been in action before. Here's P. & A. Campbell's *Cambria, converted into a minesweeper in World War One, one of the 'butterfly boats' that impressed the Navy.*

This is the way 'Galloping Gertie' – the Glen Gower – did her wartime job. Exhausted soldiers snatched from the Dunkirk beaches.

then south at such speed that flames 20 feet high belched from the funnel. After more supplies in Harwich it was off to Dunkirk.

'It was like going down Piccadilly. We were in a long stream of boats of all sorts.' Gertie slowed to a trot to go in close to the shore, but the weight of

the extra coal made her much lower in the water than usual. She ran aground. While she sat there the crew lowered the boats and rowed ashore to pick up soldiers. Others reached Gertie by swimming or floating out on planks or cans but most were in the boats designed to carry 26 but this time taking 50, exhausted men flopped inside or clinging to the sides. Just one small problem. How to get Gertie back into deep water? Along came Gerties's old mate *Waverley,* renamed the *Snaefell,* and although she, too,was packed with troops she hauled Gertie away.

With 600 men aboard Gertie was on her way, but as she neared the harbour entrance she was ordered to pick up more men at the quayside. Well, she'd done it a thousand times before at Cardiff's Pier Head – but not with shells exploding all round while ominous columns of smoke rose from beaches about as far away as the Ship and Pilot had been from that Pier Head in happier times.

But, recalled Edward Rees, 'There were a couple of trawlers near us and the casual attitude of their crews bucked us up no end. They were just leaning over the side, spitting into the water. They didn't seem in any hurry at all.' Then a shell burst under Gertie's stern and another smashed through the deck, exploding among troops

Meanwhile the end comes for the Glen Gower, *immortalised as Galloping Gertie. Here she is being towed out of Penarth Dock in 1960.*

crammed into the stokers' quarters. Ten men died and six were injured. War had come with a vengeance to our pleasure steamer.

While all this was happening more troops were piling aboard and as Gertie steamed out she passed the *Brighton Belle*, only her funnels showing above the water. It was like seeing one of the family laid out...

And out in the Channel where she'd frolicked so often, this time on her last journey to Antwerp where she would be broken up, a lone yachtsman saying farewell.

Gertie got back to Harwich with 1,500 men aboard, her flag at half mast in honour of the dead below decks. But there was no time for a break. 'They patched us up, coaled us, gave us extra food and blankets. Then we were off again.'

Joining Gertie on that second trip were more playmates from that fun-filled past, echoing balmy days when the only danger was floating driftwood. There they were, the *Cambria* and the *Westward Ho* and the *Britannia*, all bound for the battered Dunkirk beaches. For Gertie it was back to Harwich with another 700 men then, after more coal, a third trip. As they crossed the Channel they saw flights of RAF planes overhead. A wonderful sight: maybe the Germans would get a taste of what they'd been dishing out. No time to investigate, though, not with another 600 men waiting. Among them were Guardsmen who sat, and Edward Rees looked on with astonishment, who actually sat there as Gertie dodged the shells on her way back – polishing their boots.

He never forgot the way they left Gertie. 'They marched off, ramrod straight.' No slipshod shamble down the gangplank for the Guards.

Well, the Welsh Navy suffered at Dunkirk. The *Brighton Belle* and the *Brighton Queen* both sank after hitting wreckage while the *Devonia* was bombed just off the beach. Two more would go before war's end: the *Snaefell*, the *Waverley* of more tranquil times sunk off West Hartlepool; the *Glen Avon* after foundering during the Normandy landings.

And Galloping Gertie? In 1960 she made her last sad crossing. To a Belgian yard where she was broken up like the *Glen Usk*, the *Cambria*, *Westward Ho* and *Britannia*, leaving nothing but their names to history.

By the summer of 1961, as the docks themselves looked in terminal decline, only three paddle steamers were left. Just 20 years later the White Funnel Fleet followed the Red and Yellow Funnels into the world's attic.

Tatem and Tommy: Two Dock Immortals

SO where were we before we met up with Galloping Gertie?

We left Cardiff in 1920, a year after the riots, a year when in spite of the 400 ships registered in the docks, the sharper operators could sniff the winds of change. And among the sharpest was our old friend Bill Tatem, now, of course, Lord Glanely. So let's look at the man who can lay claim to being the most colourful Docksman of 'em all.

He was born in Appledore, North Devon, in 1868 and after a couple of years at sea during which he experienced a shipwreck and Yellow Fever he opted, with sound common sense, for a less stressful life, turning up in Cardiff where he became a junior clerk with a firm of tugboat owners. Inevitably, he branched out on his own and on 14 September 1897, two months after taking delivery of his first ship, the *Lady Lewis*, he married Ada Mary Williams, of Pengam Farm, Cardiff. On her maiden voyage the 2,950 ton vessel was commanded by a man whose name, like Tatem's, would become part of Cardiff folkore – Captain William Reardon-Smith. Their lives were also linked in another way – by one of those odd quirks of fate, both men would be given the Freedom of the City of Cardiff on 23 March 1928.

But back to those early years. By 1905 Tatem had 14 ships and he would never look back. So why did those other Docksmen on the day the king came to Cardiff label him 'ignorant, rough and uncouth' while others accused him of being illiterate? Even the working men on the docks, men who'd seen him only from a distance joined in: one anonymous trimmer from Cogan, when asked what he thought of the great man, replied

simply, 'He's a jumped-up so-and-so.' You have to put it down to envy. For Tatem was the boldest of a buccaneering breed. When his docks were a swarming, dusty, clamourous, cash-clinking cornucopia he was king. Because he was a character. And he might have invented that slogan, 'If you've got it, flaunt it.' He flaunted it in a way that endeared him to the dockers. He

Here he is, the legendary Bill Tatem – now Lord Glanely – as he leads in Singapore, winner of the 1930 St Leger.

And this is how the local newspaper announced his triumph when his horse Grand Parade won the 1919 Derby at 33-1. Unfortunately most Docksmen and dockers put their money on his other horse Dominion.

became a racehorse owner, a member of the exclusive Jockey Club, a giant of the turf with, eventually, a massive mansion in that Mecca of all racing devotees, Newmarket. It took him only ten years to become a Derby-winner, but in the 1960s and 1970s you could still hear old dockers moan that Tatem had doubled-crossed them. How? Well let's step back to those docks in the summer of 1919...

Word filters down, perhaps by way of some of Tatem's business pals after lunches in the Exchange. 'It's Dominion for the Derby... Bill Tatem says it's a cert.'

In turn the whisper spreads, 'It's Dominion for the Big 'Un,' and in the Packet and the Pilot and the Freemasons and the Mountstuart the dockers and the trimmers write out their slips and as the bookies' runners move into the Bay the whispers get louder and more cash is handed over for this, well this is going to be the big Cardiff coup. So they all sit back waiting to collect from their 100-9 sure thing. It has to be. Tatem is tipping it.

And yes, Tatem's horse wins. Unfortunately for those dockers, those trimmers, those seamen and the Docksmen, he wins with his other, unfancied horse. Grand Parade finishes at a mouth-watering 33-1 but it seems that... *nobody is on it.*

Tatem would not have been popular when the tycoons met for lunch in Culley's, the renowned restaurant in the Exchange basement where 3s 6d would buy a Dover sole 'hanging over the edge of the plate', with a bottle of wine to wash it down. You can almost hear the rumours – 'Must have won a million. At that price.'

In Culley's, incidentally, the Docksmen dressed distinctively, always aware of 'image'. They wore silk hats and spats and carried canes. Some wore frock coats and it's said that one man was thrown out of the building for daring to go in sporting check breeches and leggings. The cad. Anyway, in that pivotal year when Tiger Bay was tearing itself apart, Bill Tatem won over £30,000 in prize money, finishing first in the list of winning owners, and besides his Derby winner seven of his horses won at Royal Ascot where he was doubtless the envy of all the toffs. Over the years he'd win all five Classics picking up more than a quarter of a million pounds in prize money. And he was shrewd enough the year after his turf triumph to sell his entire fleet – while others like the unfortunate Gould were buying themselves a place on the road to ruin. No wonder he left

Tommy Letton – Tommy the Fish – one of Cardiff's immortals, doing his rounds in the Bay.

millions when he died in 1942 during a bomb attack on Weston-super-Mare, the 'safe' town to which he retired, during World War Two. He was a true docks legend.

And so, in a way, was Tommy Letton.

He didn't leave a fortune but his name lives on around the docks and Tiger Bay in more ways than one. For there's now a Letton Road in the new Bay, immortalising the man who, like Dublin's Molly Malone, wheeled his wheelbarrow through streets broad and narrow for close to 50 years. Like Molly he was a fishmonger and, by another of those coincidences, he started pushing his barrow around the Bay in that milestone year of 1920. He'd fill his barrow with fish from the famous Neale and West Trawlers – another thread in the tapestry of docks history – and there were plenty of people who didn't eat till Tommy turned

up. Why? Because Tommy would wait for his money, that's why, cycling round on a Saturday morning collecting what was owing, even waiting for husbands to come home from sea if cash was short. So, road or no road, he will live forever in Bay legend as Tommy the Fish. But did his father really play with Bill Tatem's father in years gone by?

That's part of the Letton family legend. – Tommy's older sister Beatrice always swore that 'Tatem came to live in the docks as a boy. And he played with my father.'

Perhaps just another piece of dockland apocrypha, but Beatrice offers an ironic counterpoint to the jubilant songs of the Docksmen. She was 14 years old in 1910, the year Captain Scott came to Cardiff to collect his thousand pounds donation at a single sitting. But she was earning sixpence for

And here he is at the age of 88, posed proudly beside the sign making him a part of the Bay's history. As a tribute the city renamed Schooner Way running off Bute Street, Letton Road.

spending her Saturday morning scrubbing the stairs and landings of a four storey building.

'We didn't have any money then so I thought I'd give my brothers and sisters a party. I bought a pound and a half of slab cake at fourpence a pound. I thought my mother would be proud.'

But cake, far away from the tables of the tycoons' mansions, was a luxury to be avoided.

'I went home with the cake, and my mother hit me from the front door to the back. We needed money, not slab cake.' You think of the £500 handed over by Daniel Radcliffe, and then of sixpen'orth of slab cake. You could have bought an awful lot of slab cake for five hundred quid. Beatrice started work young. When she started washing clothes she had to stand on a stool at the sink, spending nine hours a day at it, for the princely sum of 1s 6d.

But she still had time to savour the sights and sounds of the docks. 'There'd be dice games on the pavements and pitch and toss at the back of the Mount Stuart Dry Docks… and music and singing from the pubs. They all had pianos and they'd be rolled out on to the streets at Christmas and New year's Eve.'

She remembered hanging out of the window, ten years old as everyone assembled at the Pier Head, ships' hooters signalling the start of 1906. 'And there were German bands in the summer and the little kids would be dancing to them in the streets… and sometimes we'd see the millionaires go by, men in top hats, the Docksmen.' She looked back down the years to see Mr Towler, the caretaker of the Sailors' Home who kept chickens and sold eggs.

'We used to love going for eggs. We could look in and see the little cubicles where the sailors slept.' Mr Towler took his duties seriously. He'd lecture his sailors. 'Now don't ever insult one of those children or the women. They're decent, respectable people.' And no one, Beatrice said long, long years after Mr Towler's death, 'No one ever did.'

Just a tiny fragment of docks' history remembered in very old age by a lady whose own history spanned the great years. Yet it shows the enormous gulf between the Haves and the Have-nots in those years when Cardiff was the Coal Capital of the World.

And of course, we know when they were: from, say, the 1880s to the the most miraculously bountiful year of all, 1913. So before moving on to the General Strike when we'll see battleships in the Channel and steel-helmeted troops in Tiger Bay, let's pause to reflect on the changing life and times of the place where we began in 1858 – Loudoun Square.

The Bay's Own Long John Silver

SO WHERE, you wonder, is Mrs James Cowell, teacher of French, on this day in 1882? Change indeed, for here at her No. 8 we find Mrs Mary Thomas, lodging housekeeper. Seamen's lodgings next door as well, with Mrs Eliza Jeffries in charge. And what of Miss Eliza Pincott's Seminary for Young Ladies? All gone, and Mr Harry Saunderson, cab driver now lives there. A reminder that all transport is horse-drawn and that the only thing you don't get from the ancient papers and directories charting the remorseless march of the years is the smell that must have been all pervading. But what's the betting that Harry had the best rhubarb in the Square? At No. 54 is Captain Charles Lindbergh, master mariner. Years later there would be speculation after the famous Lindbergh kidnapping that there was a family connection, and yes, the legendary airman Charles Lindbergh did come to Wales in the 1930s. Except for Mr Witzen, mariner, and Stefano K. Cravos, all own Anglo-Saxon names and some of the old prestige lingers: for no fewer than six master mariners live on the Square along with Edgar D. Jones, surgeon and our old acquaintance John Greatrex, broker. And here's the Revd J. Arthur Jones, among the mechanics and mariners, the sailmaker, the boiler maker, the salesman and marine engineer.

So they watched the docks grow – and moved out.

The names looking up from the faded street directory of 1913 tell the story. What do we find where Stefano K. Cravos lived just 30 years before? Why, Mr Jeremiah Dixon's boarding house for Borstal Boys. Perhaps it's just as well that Miss Eliza Pincott's Young Ladies are long

gone. Meanwhile, John Greatrex's home is now Mrs O'Leary's boarding house next door to Ibrahim Mahomed's Arab lodging house. And on the other side, where James Gordon Thomas, clerk, lived in 1882, we find Mr Lan-Chow who runs, yes, another boarding house. As do Adolfo Gonzalez, D. Sarakinos, A. Nicolai, and C. Sevieri. But not a master mariner left although there's still a surgeon at No. 46, D.W. Girvan taking the place of Dr Edgar D. Jones. There would be even greater changes in the years to come – but we'll pay a return visit to Loudoun Square before they flatten all the fine old houses in the 1960s: and maybe find out who were last to live in Miss Pincott's and Mrs Cowell's and Mr Greatrex's abodes.

But back to 1913 when, to get the real flavour of the docks and Tiger Bay, you have to go to the most storied street of all, before taking a walk to the dock gates. To Bute Street. And James Street.

The names sing off the pages, summoning images of souks and far off seashores, and for romantics it's all as enchanted and exotic as the Silk Road to Samarkand, as packed with wonders as Aladdin's cave. Until you meet a name like Edward England, importer of (of all things) potatoes, to break the spell. When it comes to wonder, what chance has a name like Edward England, potato importer, got against, say, Socrates Ambatielos or his neighbours Smile Mahomet and Pascal Bernasconi, or H.C. de Martins Pinheiro and Manuel Donizo. In 1882 the most arresting name had been Cornelius Driscoll of the Irish Harp Tavern, but since then they've flooded in from every point of the compass to make Bute Street the most

1 May 1926, and the South Wales Echo *breaks the news of the General Strike.*

cosmopolitan corner not just of Cardiff but of the country. Asylum-seekers? The term hadn't been invented then.

So here we have them, dozens of boarding houses for every race, cafes with discreet upstairs rooms, 'refreshment houses,' like Ahmed Abraham's, perhaps with secret places behind gauze curtains; and restaurants and pubs like the Crown kept by Mr Tom Dancer, and little shops selling everything from sweet potatoes and volcanic curry powder to seamen's jerseys and chew tobacco. But dominating everything are the shipping offices, at least 50 of them – from the Clyde Shipping Company to the famous Radcliffe's vast operation. And one after the other, the colliery agents and the coal exporters sit shoulder to shoulder next to giants like Guest, Keen & Nettlefold's and Cory Brothers and even the Brazilian Coal Company Ltd. Here's the Canadian Pacific Railway and – a name to conjure up visions of golden beaches, dusky maidens and breeze-blown palm trees – The Imperial West India Mail Service Co Ltd.

If you want even more proof that Cardiff in this year of 1913 is among the world's high fliers, why, consider the countries paying court by sending their representatives – all here on Bute Street. Consuls from Belgium, The Netherlands, Russia

(while the Tsar still ruled); Portugal, Brazil and the Dominican Republic; France and Norway and Greece, national flags flying over the pavement, more gaudy pieces in the kaleidoscopic jigsaw that is Bute Street.

And what of James Street, running right up to the dock gates, in this year when it was claimed that if you swung a bucket over your head you'd collect enough coaldust to bank up the fire, so thick were the clouds drifting down from the docks? More shipping offices and coal exporters, of course, but here you got a real sniff of the sea. How? Why, simply by gazing into shop windows that made you feel you were off to foreign parts. For you'd see sextants and compasses, seaboots and jerseys, telescopes and jaunty peaked caps, all the paraphernalia needed to get you round the Horn and plenty of insurance brokers to make sure you were covered in case of disaster.

F. Primavesi sold china – and guns. G.W. Lennox sold maps, some, you like to think, marking out the most forlorn spots on earth, giving glimpses of such wonders as the Mindaneo Deep or the site of lost Atlantis. And, showing us what a different place the old earth was in 1913, at number 70, in Boston Buildings, you'd find the representative of the Austro-Hungarian Empire. It's as remote to us now as the Roman Empire, but its Archduke's death just a year on would bring the war to change everything. Oh yes, in Pembroke Buildings, you'd also find the Man from Peru. No, not the Pru. Another consul from a far-off land paying court in Cardiff. And, of course, there were the Ship and Pilot and the White Hart, pubs that have seen it all, that have watched the captains and the coal kings depart, and still sit on their corners. These days, no windows bursting with seamen's jerseys. Just little houses.

In that year of 1913 if you walked right to the end of Bute Street you would reach Solly Andrews' Coffee Tavern and on any given morning it's likely that you'd come across Frank Spray or Alfred Howells, Jim Phillips or Billy

The name sounded familiar – Special Constable Edward Churchill (centre) with the volunteer crew of a Cardiff bus during the strike. You can see why striking dockers called them 'the plus fours brigade' as the buses sailed down Bute Street with that 'prominent Cardiff man' aboard taking joy rides.

Hughes sampling the great Solly's product. For they were dock gatemen, men who actually lived with their families on the dock itself only yards away from the Coffee Tavern. And there was another gateman named Ben Davies whose son Percy was born inside these dock gates in 1905, the year when Wales beat the first mighty All Black rugby team. And thereby, as they say, hangs a tale. Or, given that Percy would grow up to become one of the most remarkable raconteurs even the docks or Tiger Bay has seen (Oscar Wilde or Peter Ustinov themselves would have given ground), thereby hangs several dozen tales.

But before turning Percy loose with his thoughts on the immortal Bob Downey (the Bay's own Long John Silver) let's see how the events beginning on 1 May 1926, affected him, personally. May Day, the workers' day, traditionally a time for miners and their mates to celebrate beneath the brave flutter of bright Lodge banners, a time for parades and pledges of better times to come. That hopeful visionary Robert Owen had proclaimed May Day the day for the start of a new millennium, the beginning of earthly paradise for the workers. But almost a century had passed since his hopeful vision and on this May Day there were only apocalyptic visions. This May Day, many felt, signalled not the start of some fine new millennium but the beginning of an industrial Armageddon. It began with a lockout of miners refusing to take pay cuts while working longer hours and inevitably became a nationwide strike called by the TUC.

As always in South Wales, the miners were the shock troops of this latest battle between Labour and Capital, and battle it was. The *Echo* informed readers that the Emergency Act brought into force gave the Government 'drastic powers'. The Government had prepared as though for war, or revolution. And again, as always, that link between miners and dockworkers showed it had lost none of its strength. At a special meeting members of the Coaltrimmers' Union in the South Wales ports pledged 'support to the miners in their struggle... and promises all the moral and active support we are capable of rendering.'

Terms like 'battle' and 'war' might seem over the top but not when you read the Home Office Report on the first day of the strike, the authorities clearly targeting Cardiff and its docks. 'All continues quiet. It is hoped to run the Corporation buses in Cardiff tomorrow.' Then the news that showed how determined the Government was. 'A submarine arrived in Cardiff today and a cruiser is expected tomorrow. Several potato boats are to be unloaded by non-union labour.' Then, ominously, 'Adequate protection has been arranged.'

On 5 May, 200 special constables began patrolling the streets while four warships, *Simoon*, *Tetrarch*, *Caledon* and *Cleopatra* steamed into the Bristol Channel to prevent any stoppages in the ports. The cruiser *Cleopatra* tied up in Cardiff docks while potato boats, once unloaded by women, were handed over to non-union labour. On the night of 5 May the BBC, taking a stance so one-sided that even its regal boss John Reith confessed he felt like asking for his licence money back, reported that 'Cardiff Docks were in full swing'. Steel-helmeted troops marched through the docks as Captain Arthur Evans, MP for Cardiff South, was assuring the Commons that public opinion in South Wales was solidly behind the Government. The Cardiff Strike Bulletin promptly retorted that by public 'the misrepresentative for Cardiff South probably means the members of the Baltic Exchange at Cardiff Docks....'

And the *South Wales Echo*, no Cap'n Tupper around to provide stories, sided with that 'misrepresentative'. The latest in a long line of Men About Town talked of a May Day when 'Caliban had been let loose to work his evil purpose. In the name of liberty and democracy men were denied the most elementary rights of thought and action, means of travel and work.' Still, the men referred to sardonically by the strikers as 'the plus-fours brigade' kept the trams and buses moving and at least one 'prominent Cardiff man' came closer to Tiger Bay than usual because of them. The *Western Mail* reported that 'showing his appreciation of the volunteer workers' he spent an entire morning taking 'joy rides between St Mary Street and the Pier Head'. Some of those volunteer workers were pulled off the trams they manned and there were battles in the streets of Cardiff and around the docks. One 49-year-old mother got a month's hard labour for bunging a brick through a tramcar window. And in the middle of it all was young Percy Davies, celebrating his 21st birthday in the year of the General Strike.

Percy Davies returns to the Pier Head in 1986, some 60 years after he found himself on strike and unable to go home to his mother's house inside the dock gates. So much had changed 'it broke my heart'. He never went back and died that same year.

'I am the only striker ever asked to picket his own house,' Percy would reflect in old age. He was on picket duty outside the dock gates – his mother could see him from the house inside those gates. 'I couldn't go home for the entire nine days and they wouldn't even let my mother bring clean clothes out to me. I used to sleep in any shed available, dreaming of my nice warm bed. And my mother's stew and apple tarts.'

Percy's father had to keep working as the house where they lived was tied to the job. It couldn't be risked. 'So that strike broke up families and things would never really be the same.'

It ended in the docks after nine days, although the miners would stay out for months. And those once-great docks would continue to decline. Sixty years after, with a new era dawning, Percy Davies went down to the docks and wandered the Bay for the first time since the coal had stopped coming down from the Rhondda. So how did he find his old stamping ground?

'It broke my heart. I won't go back again.'

He never did, and died in 1986, his pledge to himself kept. But Percy, like so many others who remembered the glory days, never really stopped going back. He didn't go by bus or train to Bute Street Station. He travelled, he said, 'first class by mind power.' So he saw his docks, the place where he had briefly kept a pub, always as they had been, frozen forever in a sort of marvellous, multi-coloured, pub-singing, garlic-flavoured, curry scented amber. He'd take his ticket and the final destination would be – Nostalgiaville. There was plenty to be nostalgic about and for Percy, journey's end was always a visit with Bob Downey. Percy had been a copper in the Rhondda and he'd sat over pub fires late at night drinking in tales of the mighty mountain fighters who had become legends. But you know, he'd say, 'I reckon Bob Downey would have given any of 'em a go.' That from a man who himself had been a good amateur heavyweight.

The name resonates down the unforgiving years. If ever there was a King of Tiger Bay, they'll tell you, Bob Downey owned the crown. Percy was just a lad when he met him for the first time. As we said, his father worked and lived inside the dock gates and Percy had to do his bit, which meant closing the gates across the road when an engine was ready to shunt by.

'I'd be on the gate ready to close it when I'd hear this yell – 'Leave 'em be, boy' – and this big frightening fellow on a horse and cart would come thundering through on his way to pick up a load of sawdust.' Percy confessed that he was terrified. 'I'd hold those gates open all right and wouldn't

give the engine driver the signal to start until the cart was through. I always got a shilling thrown at me, always, but it wasn't the shilling, it was the fear of what would happen if I closed 'em.'

That was Bob Downey, the Sawdust King, owner of an infamous killer crutch, on one of his missions. But sawdust was only part of his empire. Percy always thought of him as King of the Bay but for another boy from the Bay he was 'a dead ringer for Long John Silver', George Johnson remembered, 'right down to the wooden crutch and parrot.' He used to hang the parrot outside his pub, the Bute Castle, and taught him to recognise one of the men on the Downey black list, a bald old police inspector. According to Bay legend the bird would stare stonily down at the hundreds of passers-by, uttering not a squeak, not a squawk, not a blink of beady eye. Until the inspector marched by. Then he would give the embarrassed copper some five minutes of high-class cursing, enough to make a bosun blush, with particular reference to the parenthood of most policemen and the baldness of this particular one. No one messed with Bob Downey.

'Any arguments,' said Percy, 'and he'd crack you over the side of the head with his crutch. He was a brute of a man.' Other awed old-timers recalled Downey vaulting over the bar of his pub and clearing the room inside a couple of minutes if there was a fight. Percy remembered him as fearless. 'He'd deal with the toughest seamen and the way he used that crutch at close quarters had to be seen to be believed. He only had one leg. God knows what he would have done if he'd had a full complement.'

He was the archetypal 'sporting landlord' around since Regency days when the bareknuckle battlers would meet in the yard of some country pub. And Downey was the first trainer and manager of one of the immortals of prizefighting, Peerless Jim Driscoll himself. Jim was born in Newtown, just off Bute Street, and one day he was down at the stadium on the Marl, the field on the banks of the Taff across from the docks, when Downey appeared to see how his trotters were performing – yes, he was a racing man as well.

He spotted Jim, a cigarette in one hand, a girl on the other, and instantly jumped off his horse, swung his crutch, and knocked the cigarette out of Driscoll's hand. There'd be none of that, he snapped, then, with a glare at the girl, none of that, either. Then he gave Driscoll the sack shouting 'You'll never get another backer after me.' That's the story told to Bill Barrett, local historian born and bred in the docks. Percy Davies, who saw Driscoll fight, said that Downey and Driscoll resumed their friendship as Bob kept up his interest in what he no doubt termed the Noble Art. He ran a string of boxers who worked for him, delivering that famous sawdust to butchers' shops and pubs – in those days when the sawdust mopped up the booze and blood on the bar room floor.

'They were more frightened of him than they were of any opponent.' But it was Downey's horses that Percy always remembered most fondly as he looked back down the years. 'Marvellous trotting ponies, they were. Real high-steppers. And he also kept a lot of dogs.'

What else but… bull terriers. Downey was a man ahead of his time when you think of the pit bulls (those 'pets' mostly called Tyson) that caused consternation by killing a couple of dozen people in the United States. They earned the reputation of being killing machines with the bite of a crocodile but Downey wouldn't have been intimidated – 'He was afraid of nothing and nobody.'

And he's also part of another Bay legend – the Hotel de Marl. In days when the chapels ruled and the city shut down on the Sabbath you couldn't get a drink in a Cardiff pub. Until the resourceful landlord of the Glendower, at the other end of Crichton Street from Bute Street, realised that his licence allowed him to sell food and drink to bona fide travellers on a Sunday.

Word spread. Drinkers flooded in from all points, so many of them that they were selling out of train tickets for the trip from Penarth. It had to stop when the police threatened to take his licence.

Enter Bob Downey – in a song written by Mike Johnson, balladeer of the Bay. It's called, naturally, Hotel de Marl and you'll soon know why. No Sunday sales of beer but… well let Mike Johnson tell us:

'And in the Bute Tavern with a pint of good brew, the Conspirators huddled (the way plotters do). And it didn't take more than an hour or two to decide who was buying the next round. Then Downey got drunk, and he had an idea: How about it if we buy a few barrels of beer, on a Saturday night without any fear, We can drink 'em on Sunday, – (AH-AH).

They did. They carried the barrels down to the Marl – the field where Downey exercised his trotters – and stood guard all night. Then on Sunday it was opening time as usual with Downey in charge. It didn't last long. The end of the Hotel de Marl meant that Downey's customers made the long walk to the Carpenter's Arms at the top of Rumney Hill, just inside Monmouthshire and therefore able to open on a Sunday. Percy Davies had seen it all but the fact that Bob Downey left such an indelible impression tells us that here was a somewhat special character. And plenty of other old timers in the Bay would talk about this madman who some of them called Uncle Bob. Yet for all his tales of pub fights and cranium-cracking crutches, Percy always insisted that the Bay wasn't a violent place – if you minded your own business.

'If we went into town my mother would warn us not to miss the last tram. She believed all the stories. But I always missed the last tram and I always walked home down Bute Street and nothing ever happened.' The town centre in the 1920s and 1930s was a more dangerous place. 'Look sideways at someone in the Albert and you'd get a punch. There were tough men there in those days. Compared to that, pub life in Tiger

Bay was peaceable. My sisters could walk all round the place without trouble.'

Bob Downey's name, then, is enshrined forever in Bay history. But there were others, plenty of others. Men like John Purveau, known as Father Purveau, reputed to be the oldest man in the Bay. He earned his fame by officiating at Tiger Bay funerals, dancing besides the hearse while wearing top hat and tailcoat, carrying a silver handled cane. He kept a boarding house and at one time was branch president of an organisation called the Negro Universal Improvement Association. The people of the Bay who remembered him are long gone, but years ago they'd recall him as a 'peacemaker,' the man brought in to cool down tempers when trouble brewed. He's remembered, now, every time someone sings Mike Johnson's song The Hymn of Father Purveau.

' See the black-plumed horses in the funeral parade, pulling curtained coaches out of Windsor Esplanade, As the ships' horns blare over Cardiff Bay, saying: 'Here comes Father Purveau.'

Father Purveau was the other side of the Bay coin from villains like Shanghai Walsh, and there was another character just as fondly remembered – regarded as something of a saint. They used to say that if you sent a letter from the other side of the world addressed, simply, 'Uncle Ike, Cardiff,' he'd get it.

Uncle Ike? That's what they called Isaac Phenis, one of the leading lights of the Gospel Mission Hall on Angelina Street. Before they opened the Mission Uncle Ike used to hold services in his boarding house on South Church Street and they'd claim in the Bay that so many people turned up they had to sit on the stairs and look through the windows. Uncle Ike turned no one away and in the scullery – he called it his galley – there was always a huge saucepan of pea soup bubbling away on the fire. It was said that the police used to send down-and-outs round to Uncle Ike for a meal and they always got bread and soup – and never had to sing a hymn for their supper. They'd usually stay for the service but you have to wonder whether it was spiritual sustenance or the more substantial stuff from the galley that kept them coming. Old men who remembered Uncle Ike mused that yes, some people did exploit his good nature but he never seemed concerned. He died with nothing, but as someone who knew him well once remarked, 'He was rich with the Lord, and got his reward in Heaven.'

And then there was the claimant to Bob Downey's title – although they called Peter Link the King of the Africans. He was another boarding house master who looked after the interests of his people, a man of great dignity who would go to the shipping office to ensure that African seamen got their rights. Cardiff had a council and Tiger Bay had its councillors but it was men like Uncle Ike, Father Purveau and Peter Link who had the trust – and with Uncle Ike, the love – of the people.

From Vic and Joe: Final Farewells to the Bay

REMEMBER Father Purveau and you remember the funerals of Tiger Bay – in truth, they can never really be forgotten for there was always something special about them, particularly in days when the black-plumed horses hauled the hearse, when, at times, a little bit of New Orleans came to Cardiff.

A couple have gone into Bay folklore – for vastly different reasons. One was, well, if you can call a funeral comic, this was it. The other was truly mystical. The comic? They used to talk about a one-legged Bute Street cobbler who died, poisoned, the locals reckoned, by a dodgy tin of salmon. No post mortem, so they put him in his coffin and then, in a sentimental gesture, added his wooden leg as the Egyptians left cherished possessions in the tomb of a Pharoah. Halfway down Bute Street something shifted the wooden

A typical Tiger Bay funeral at the turn of the last century. Note the top hats being worn but no birds following this one.

leg, which started rattling around in the box. A long gone Bay grocer who swore he was an eye witness always insisted that 'As soon as the four bearers heard the rattle from the coffin they dropped it and took off without looking back. They thought *he* was coming back.'

The cobbler eventually got to the cemetery but his departure wasn't as memorable, or lyrical as that of an old Arab who departed in truly startling style, if you can believe the tales told years later in the Bay. He lived in South Church Street and used to buy sacks of corn which he'd scatter each day for the hundreds of pigeons which congregated – maybe alerted to this regular treat by pigeon post. On the morning the old man was buried dozens of birds roosted on his coffin as it left the house, and they followed him to the cemetery, hundreds of them flying above the funeral procession, as silent as the mourners themselves

Well that's the story, and if it's been embroidered a bit over the years, it's still worth remembering, along with the cobbler and his wooden leg, as an example of how Tiger Bay could always trigger legend. But there are still thousands of people who vividly remember the funeral of one of the greatest Bay characters of all and no embroidery is needed. Vic Parker was more than a marvellous musician: he was a phenomenon, a boy from the Bay who became a true legend, and when he died in February 1978, Tiger Bay showed the world that it still knew how to say farewell to a favourite son. No Father Purveau this time, instead, in black morning dress, chief mourner Rico Dando paced in front of the coffin while a black-draped Sousaphone led a New Orleans jazz band along Bute Street.

Vic, as he'll always be remembered, singing in the Quebec Hotel on Crichton Street between the Custom House and the Glendower – all gone.

Eighty years later in 1978 the Bay says farewell to Vic Parker, one of its favourite sons, the jazz band leading the way and a team of 40 pall bearers sharing the burden.

A team of 40 pall bearers were there to take Vic on his last journey through familiar streets, changing places on the move every 50 yards. And behind them marched hundreds of his friends and fans from all over the city. They'd come to the pubs in the Bay and the docks to listen to the Master, pubs like the Quebec, gone now along with Vic and they were here now, to say, in real Bay parlance, Ta-ra Vic. After the service in the Church of St Mary the Virgin the whole of Tiger Bay danced on the Bute Street Bridge to *When the Saints Go Marching In*. And even though Vic was gone, the melody lingered on – they packed the Paddle Steamer in Loudoun Square and listened to tapes of his performances, proof, as someone or other observed that night, that people like Vic can never really go away.

Twelve years later, on another bleak February day, the Bay said its farewells to another son who had held, like Vic, a place in every one's heart. When the *South Wales Echo* reported the funeral of Joe Erskine it's headline said simply: 'As Great a Grief as Peerless Jim', and every true Cardiffian knew exactly what this meant. It meant the sort of sadness you experience when there is a death in the family. For like the great Jim Driscoll before him, Joe was not merely respected, he was loved.

When they buried Jim Driscoll – again, and this is eerie, on another chill February day in 1925 – more than 100,000 mourners lined the city streets to see him carried from a numbed Newtown to Cathays Cemetery. Newtown, the original Irish quarter, lay just off Bute Street, so again the coffin was carried along that legendary strip. Men who watched their hero depart told each other that there would never be another outpouring of collective grief to match Driscolls's farewell: never another fighter whose gloves, like Jim's, could so unerringly touch the heart of a city.

In 1990 the Bay turned out to see their boxing hero Joe Erskine on his way. Joe's cortège travelled the streets he'd loved so much and here he is in later life, with a portrait of himself in his prime.

But the biggest funeral of all was in 1925 when Peerless Jim Driscoll went to his rest. More than 100,000 mourners lined the way from Bute Street to the cemetery.

But then along came Joe. Like Peerless Jim, he had been more than a marvellous credit to the hard old game he graced with such dignity and distinction. He had been a credit to his city and his country as well, and although he went to the top of the tree he never forgot his roots; and they went deep, those roots, all the way back to his beloved Bay. He was born in Angelina Street only a few hundred yards from Driscoll's birthplace, and his love for it never wavered even though the old streets had been flattened, the old men and women moved out.

So at his own wish they carried his coffin back down that remembered road and through the little streets along the places all around: along Bute Street, of course, and few could have failed to remember Vic Parker then. So many echoes of so much sadness on that road from the city's centre to the docks. But that is the way Joe wanted it. And that is why they loved him, those old warriors with echoes of ancient battles imprinted on their faces, men come to pay tribute, gathered in the taverns of Tiger Bay and the docks and, yes, in the town centre before the funeral. Joe had earned around £80,000 in the 1950s and early 1960s – maybe a million in turn-of-the-

Jim's mother stands besides his Lonsdale Belt and other trophies with the picture of her son in typical pose.

century terms – but he died broke. Yet he was a man without malice, an envoy of the city entirely without envy.

Even in the last week of his tragically short life – he was only 56 – he could smile over an MBE and millions for Frank Bruno, a manufactured boxer who, as that other immortal, the Rhondda's Tommy Farr used to say, couldn't have hit Joe on the arse 'with a handful of rice'. So Joe could shake his head in wonder over the staggering sums the game had brought to the likes of Bruno and young Mike Tyson, and yes, then shake his head and say, 'Well, good luck to 'em.'

So again they filled St Mary the Virgin and for every sporting icon like Barry John or Henry Cooper come to bow a head for a boy from the Bay there were a hundred men and women from streets he'd known as a kid, there because Joe was 'one of us'. Patrick Williams, Dando to one and all, sang *Panis Angelicus* and *The Lord's Prayer* in a baritone that sent a shiver down every spine, that had us wondering why he wasn't up there with Bassey. And then, when Edith Bindon, small, plump, diffident in a head scarf, sang *Swing Low Sweet Chariot*, and someone mused that we had heard an angel singing, then you had to wonder just how much untapped talent had been born, had died in the Bay.

Boston, Boxers, Bassey... and the Docks' Own Olympian

WELL, some had been fulfilled. Joe himself had been British, Commonwealth and European heavyweight, recognised as the finest ring artist to come out of Cardiff since Driscoll. And among a glaxy of great sportsmen at the funeral was another Bay legend, the immortal Billy Boston.

Like Joe, he was born in Angelina Street and played in the same local rugby side, the CIACS, but unlike Joe he had to leave his beloved home town to find success. His brother Herbert once remarked that perhaps people in Cardiff needed reminding of just how great Billy was. 'They must

The great Billy Boston while doing his two years Army service in conscription days.

Billy Boston, a bit older (with less hair), in action for Wigan, the club where he earned rugby immortality.

And here with a pair of Bay Boys who also achieved sporting fame: Billy, left, with Welsh soccer international Peter Rodriguez and Clive Sullivan, another rugby league star.

regard him as the kid down the street, in Cardiff, Up in Wigan he's an idol. An idol.'

Billy, as they say in Wales, 'went North' in 1953 when he was 19 years old. To Wigan for the then enormous sum of £3,500. He'd played for Neath and Pontypridd before that but you still hear down the Bay that because of his colour he was never considered by Cardiff, the self-proclaimed World's Greatest Rugby Club. Whether it's true or not we'll probably never know, but that's the belief down the Bay and no one doubts that he would have become as big a name in Rugby Union as he was in Rugby League.

They called him the Wigan Walloper and no wonder – he scored 482 tries for the club as well as 24 for Great Britain, and, the youngest player ever selected, went on his first tour of Australia and New Zealand in 1954 after only six Rugby League games. He played in six Wembley Cup Finals and helped win three of them but looking back in 1993 he confessed that he still felt it was a tragedy he had to go North – 'Because I wanted to win a Welsh cap.' Well, Richard Burton once said he would have swapped all his fame and fortune for just one game for Wales at Number 10, but whereas he was dreaming, Billy Boston would surely have become as great a Union legend as he was in League. Great Britain's gain was Wales's most avoidable loss – if Billy Boston had been given the call by the Cardiff club would he have departed?

Billy ended his playing career with Blackpool

Docks-born Gus Risman, reckoned by some the greatest outside half Wales ever produced. He turned professional before he was 18 and Wales' loss was rugby league's gain.

And here's his son Bev, another outside half lost to Wales – he played his first Union game for England against Wales in 1959.

Borough then went on to run a pub overlooking Wigan's Central Park where he had lit the lives of so many during the 1950s and 1960s. But before Billy Boston the docks produced another giant of the game – and even Rugby Union men who saw him say he was the greatest fly half Wales ever produced. But like Newport's David Watkins, another marvellous outside half who 'went North', Gus Risman became a professional. Unlike Watkins he spent no time at all in the Union game, going to Salford as a teenager in 1929.

Gus captained Wales and the Great Britain side and picked up a cup winner's medal at Wembley at the ripe old age of 41. That was in 1952 and he played on for another two years after kicking 2,500 goals and scoring over 200 tries in his 25-year career.

For years every newspaper story referred to Gus as 'Barry-born'. In fact, he was a Docks boy whose parents moved to Barry Dock when he was a child, and it was at Barry County School that his genius was first spotted – he was not quite 18 when he turned professional.

His son Bev was a dual Union and League international and another son John was also a league international. One of Gus's biggest regrets was that he failed to sign Billy Boston when he was manager of Salford in the 1950s but the two have something unique in common – they were among the first players elected to the Rugby League Hall of Fame in 1988. The third Welshman was the greatest of them all: the immortal Jim Sullivan, Risman's idol. Gus died in 1994 but, as they say, the legend lives on in those rugby league towns far from the Docks.

'These are our trophies...' Hughie Smith, captain of CIACS, with Darren Driscoll, John Leonard, Martin Hodgkinson, Mike Hollyman, Ken Khan and Frank Fonseca, at the Cardiff and District RU annual presentation at Cardiff Athletic Club in May 1986.

Another Docks boy who went North, but in a different way, was Ryan Giggs. Yes, a Docks boy taken to Manchester by his mother when he was seven to make his name, as all the world knows, in the other game: soccer. His father Danny Williams was a superb outside half who also took to Rugby League, another in the line of sporting stars.

But talk of sport and Tiger Bay and you talk of the Cardiff International Athletic Club – the CIACS. You've heard of the Rainbow Nation. This was the original Rainbow rugby team. Tiger Bay and the Docks just after the war were, to put it mildly, short of facilities for kids. So to help fill the gap the club was founded in 1946 to keep the kids off the streets, but it didn't really begin stamping its name into the city's history until the

following year. Few could have dreamed that it would blossom into one of the finest sports clubs in Wales – what, a bunch of kids from the Docks and Tiger Bay? But who could have guessed at the untapped talent in those little streets? Joe Erskine and Billy Boston played in the same CIACS' side, earning Welsh Boys' Club caps along with Lenny Bullen and David Saleh. Youth caps went to Mike Marshall, Carl Smith and Wayne Ernest and Carl was one of three former players in the Cardiff side on the same day – Steve McCann and Martin Pengelly the others.

Besides the wondrous Joe Erskine, other top professional boxers who turned out for the team included Phil Edwards, Teddy Best and David 'Darkie' Hughes. And such was the talent that

And Hughie Smith again, this time after CIACs had won the Welsh Brewers Cup at the National Stadium in 1991.

although Billy Boston earned most publicity, so many other CIACS like Colin Dixon and Johnny Freeman 'went North' that during the early 1950s there was always a League scout or two watching the club's games. In fact, four of the CIACS went into the Cardiff Rugby League side of the 1950s – Billy Douglas, Frank Campbell, Leslie Olsen and Phil Delgardo.

During the club's great period when it was almost invincible in district rugby, for many people in South Wales the name Tiger Bay no longer spelled out intrigue and villainy (as their parents had believed). It meant – the CIACS. And given its marvellous record of promoting racial harmony it could fairly challenge its great neighbour Cardiff for the title (self-bestowed by Cardiff) of The World's Greatest Rugby Club.

Now we can't talk about sport without

recalling one of the most unlikely fighters to emerge from Tiger Bay. Prince Naseem as first Arab boxer? Forget it. In the winter of 1956 Tiger Bay had a new fighting hero to cheer – none other than Sheik Said Hassan, religious leader of the Moslem community. What a story! How the *Echo* welcomed this exotic arrival on the ring scene. 'Six hundred valley amateur boxing fans in Bargoed last night saw an Arab Sheik take part in a contest,' gasped Our Correspondent. 'And although giving away 12 pound in a cruiser weight contest, he gave a fine display of boxing which earned the approval of the packed audience.'

He was outpointed that night after winning his first fight in Ely by a knockout, but he earned so much respect from that knowledgeable crowd that they welcomed him back to Bargoed for another battle. They were disappointed. The Sheik was

The Muscular Muslim – Sheik Said Hassan, spiritual leader who also fancied his chances in the ring in 1956.

But not neglecting his duties that same year as he works on ceremonial robes.

retired from the amateur ranks after the Welsh ABA discovered that he wore contact lenses in the ring. They reached for the rulebook and announced that as Article 9a, Paragraph 4, prohibited one-eyed boxers, the same rule applied to contact lenses.

But they added: 'The Welsh ABA state that they reached their decision with regret as they did not wish to debar a man of the Sheik's standing from the sport.'

Sheik Said Hassan returned to his Tiger Bay flock and was in the news once more a couple of years later when his wife Galila Ahmed arrived from the Yemen. At the airport he persuaded her to remove her veil, as she stepped into a new life as the only woman from the Yemen – apart from the wife of the Yemeni consul in London – living in Britain at that time.

So there you are. You've heard of Muscular Christians. Trust the Bay to provide its very own Muscular Muslim.

Plenty of great sportsmen, then, from the docks and Tiger Bay. But the greatest of them all in terms of achievement must be Paulo Radmilovich. In an era of TV and media hype it was inevitable that Steve Redgrave would win world headlines for his feat of winning gold in five successive Olympics. But 'Raddy', born in Cardiff's dockland, collected four gold medals in five successive games and would probably have won another had the arrival

But is this the greatest sportsmen ever to come from the city's docks? Paulo Radmilovich, wonder swimmer, seen here in 1930 before leaving for the first Empire Games in Hamilton when he was over 40 years old.

And here he is, still spry at 70 in 1957, 12 years before his death.

of World War One not halted things. He started in the unofficial Olympics in Athens when he was 20 years old and then in 1908 at the London Olympics was one of the gold-winning 800 metres relay team.

After that he specialised in water polo, adding a polo medal to his relay gold in 1908, and earning others in 1912 and 1920. He even took part in the Empire Games of 1930 at the ripe old age – for a swimmer – of 44. Five years before that he won every British free style swimming title except for the quarter mile. Incredibly, everything else from 100 yards to five miles belonged to him and he also won the long distance championship of England – 18 years after winning it for the first time. You wonder whether Raddy learned to swim in the old sea lock! But for once the word 'legend' isn't an exaggeration, about the only Cardiff swimmer who might have rivalled him was Billy the Seal. Raddy's genius was recognised as such by the swimming world when he was the first Briton elected to the International Swimming Hall of Fame in 1967: Captain Webb, the first man to swim the English Channel, was the only other swimmer from Britain to join Raddy there.

Raddy was also a scratch golfer, a fine soccer player and a boxer of some renown. And he took up bowls at the ripe old age of 71 after retiring to run a restaurant in Weston-super-Mare where he died in 1968 at the age of 82.

Well, they could fight and they could play rugby and swim, and as we saw with Dando, they could sing. But without doubt the most famous chanteuse to come out of those streets is the woman they call the Tigress from Tiger Bay – of course, Shirley Bassey. You'll find plenty of Cardiffians who still insist she was born in Splott – let's face it, a much less romantic-sounding birthplace than Tiger Bay. But whatever, or wherever, there's no doubting that the girl Cardiffians call Our Shirl put Tiger Bay back on the map in a different way. No one needs to be told what a huge star she became but the voice was evident from the start when she worked in Currans factory – the destination, you might recall, of that 'Fu Manchu' we met many pages back. She's now Dame Shirley and for some headline writers no longer the Temptress from Tiger Bay but the Diva from the Docks.

Yet it could all have ended before she had hardly begun to climb that ladder to the very top. You can imagine the reaction in the Bay when they saw, in the biggest headlines the *Echo* could get hold of: SHIRLEY BASSEY HOTEL PRISONER.

It looked like the sort of publicity stunt Hollywood had been pulling for years. Aye, aye, mused the more cynical of her old neighbours, it's Our Shirl up to her tricks again. After all, she'd been making news ever since taking showbiz by storm. But never like this. It was like something out of a TV soap before soaps had even arrived on the scene. For this was November 1957 – three years before *Coronation Street* introduced us to Ena Sharples and the rest. Shirley Bassey, fascinated readers learned, had been held prisoner in her suite in London's Cumberland Hotel by a man so obsessed with her that he used a gun to keep her behind barricaded doors as he poured out his thoughts.

'*I love you. And if I can't have you, no one else will...*'

Melodramatic? Or what. But it was really happening and outside those bolted doors armed police were poised for a rescue act as Shirley, as she later described it, went through 'the two most terrifying hours of my life.' The terror began at 12.45 am as she sorted out the dresses she'd need for a forthcoming tour of Australia. A man rushed in, bundled two men from the dress shop out into the corridor, and then wounded a friend of Shirley's in a struggle.

For those 'two terrifying hours' the alarming visitor waved his gun and repeated, 'Shirley, I love you, I love you.' Adding to the feeling of imminent mayhem was the fact that he kept swigging from a bottle of whisky – threatening after each gulp that he would kill the singer. Then, at 2.45, he suddenly pushed Shirley out of the room and slipped back behind locked doors. Police waited another hour before smashing their way in to arrest a 20-year-old commercial traveller who promptly shot himself in the leg. After he was taken to hospital Shirley confessed that she had known the man for about a year and had once agreed to marry him – 'But only because he was very ill. I only said I would to make him better.' Two months earlier, she explained, he had been in a car crash, sustaining brain damage. 'Before the accident he was sweet and charming. I think the accident changed him.'

Two months later her unwelcome visitor was in the dock at the Old Bailey. His illness didn't save him. He was sentenced to three years in prison, after repeating yet again from the dock, 'I am devoted to her.'

The unsentimental prosecuting counsel, the legendary Christmas Humphries, simply called him 'a silly, lovesick youth'. And the Judge, Mr Justice Cassels observed in his summing up: 'You were within a hair's breadth of standing trial for

Spot the star of the future. She's in the back row.

what would have been a charge of murder.'

A hair's breadth! All that stood between Shirley Bassey and future fame, not to mention life itself.

So there you are, a suitably exciting ending to our glimpse of just a handful of the stars from a whole galaxy born and bred in our amazing corner of Cardiff.

Then, at 18, starting her career.

And here, as all the world now knows her, Shirley Bassey in full flow.

From War in Spain to War at Sea

THEY called them the Hungry Thirties and the 'little people' of the docks and Tiger Bay suffered like everybody else. But coal still dominated the docks' trade. In 1936, five years after the the world financial crisis of 1931, only two and a half per cent of exports from Cardiff were not coal or coke or patent fuel, while imports formed only 15 per cent of the total trade. World War Two would postpone the bad times, but the docks got a preview of war well before that fatal September Sunday in 1939. With hindsight we can regard the Spanish Civil War as a sort of rehearsal for the Big One. And Cardiff, with so many links to Spain, inevitably got in on the act. The Welsh connection will always be remembered for the way in which 116 miners from the valleys were among the 2,500 who went from Britain to fight fascism. They saw it as a crusade – and there had always been a great kinship between the Welsh and Spanish miners. A year before Franco's war began in July 1936, 2,000 Welsh colliers demanded the release of Spanish workers held in prisons. A week before the outbreak the fight against Fascism was already taking place in Tonypandy.

On 11 July 1936, almost 2,000 men and women from all over the Rhondda gathered at De Winton Field to break up a meeting of Oswald Mosley's Blackshirts. They swore that 'not even the ears of the sheep on the mountain shall be defiled by the words of Mosley.' Well, it wasn't Mosley delivering the message, but a man from Grangetown, a man who worked the docks – who we shall meet attempting a monumental hijack in those very docks a little later.

Anyway, 32 miners were arrested at the battle of De Winton Field and seven went to jail. One of them, Harry Dobson, emerged to ask: 'How do I get to Spain?'

He got to Spain and he died in Spain, killed on the River Ebro front in July 1938. Two years earlier he had been there at De Winton Field as John William 'Jack' O'Neill stood atop a van while bricks and bottles flew round his ears. Among his fellow Blackshirts was Tommy Moran, former middleweight champion of the Navy. Years later, in the De Winton Arms, at the back of the built-over battlefield, a man who was there recalled that summer evening. 'That Moran could go a bit... and the fellow on the van had some guts.'

Well, the fellow on the van (my brother Jack, who later served five years in the RAF) also saw the Civil War as reason for a crusade. But he and those like him regarded Francisco Franco as a true Christian knight, saving his country from

Oswald Mosley, whose lads tried to hijack the Spanish ship berthed in Cardiff Docks.

The ship that died twice, the Taffelberg, *on the beach at Barry Island.*

atheistic, church-burning, priest-killing Communists. Cardiff itself was split: in Catholic churches the prayers were for Franco, the rebel. Priests refused the sacraments to Republican sympathisers. And as in all wars, Truth was the first casualty.

So, halfway through the Spanish Civil War, we come to the battle of the Queen's Dock.

In that dock was a ship called the Christina. It belonged to a company registered in Bilbao, Sota y Azna. Two brothers owned it and, again reflecting the split in loyalties, one fought for Franco, the other for the Republic, while the ship and its crew stayed in Cardiff. And when the Rebels occupied Bilbao, the Basque capital, Cardiff's Blackshirts decided to act. Jack O'Neill remembered the battle of Queen's Dock.

'We contacted the ship's brokers and told them we would take Christina to Bilbao for the Franco forces. As far as we were concerned they agreed... so we decided to capture the ship.'

A Spanish captain with Franco sympathies was found in the docks and the Blackshirts and their crew of 'very hard lads' went down to the Queen's Dock. 'Two of us got yachting caps and wore navy blue suits. We went up the gangplank pretending to be customs officers... the rest of the men were in a railway wagon. We'd got a railwayman to bring it close to the ship.'

A sentry on the deck was overpowered, the railway wagon doors opened, and the invaders swarmed aboard and rounded up the frightened Spanish crew. Jack O'Neill was supposed to be the first mate but you realise he never got a real ticket when he recalled that 'the sharp end' of the ship pointed away from the dock exit...

News of the Christina's capture spread through the docks and a horde of angry Spaniards, most from the Basque country, stormed the ship. But they were repulsed. The Blackshirts got news to the brokers that they were ready to sail and they were, in fact, getting up steam when the Royal Navy turned up.

'An officer and four blue-jackets with fixed bayonets came aboard and took our captain off. Without the captain we had no authority to stay on the ship so we were forced off as well.'

The Blackshirts were escorted out of the docks after holding the Christina for four hours. So another odd episode in the history of this odd corner of the town had come to an end. And then, on 3 September 1939 – well, we all know what

The 'stitch up' in the Channel Dry Dock.

Bay around 25,000 ships had been in and out of Cardiff Docks, and the dockers had put in superhuman efforts to handle an average of 1,000 tons of cargo for each of those ships, including lethal cargo bound, in 1944, for the beaches of France.

As ships left, the dockers seeing them off never knew whether or not they would return. So many did not. By war's end 123 of the 164 vessels sailing from the ports had been sunk, and the blinds drawn in Tiger Bay and the Docks were not pulled because of the blackout. So many men and boys died, like Bobby Coombes, of Grangetown, just 15 when he was torpedoed on the Atlantic run. The local weekly paper reported in February 1942, that Patrick Meehan, only 17, spent 14 days in a lifeboat after being torpedoed for the second time.

We called him 'Little Billy', because Billy Andrews was truly a tiny man. No one could have guessed as he sat in Cardiff's Old Arcade pub what he had been through – though it was par for the course, perhaps, for many of the country's wartime merchant seamen. Billy was aboard the *Athelcrown* when it was torpedoed on 22 January 1942, north of Scotland. He ended in a lifeboat with 17 others, frozen and blasted by a howling gale. They had to row, the ship's carpenter, an old Shetlander, on the tiller.

'The first thing we discovered was that all the lifeboat rations had been stolen. All we had was hard-tack biscuits, pemican and water in the tanks.'

The rations had been stolen by dock workers. Yes, it happened. And in Cardiff docks as well.

Some of the survivors died and were lowered into the icy waters. Then they came across an abandoned tanker. 'A messroom boy got excited and tried to climb the mast, waving. Someone hit him on the head with a bailer to stop him but he didn't even feel it, it was so cold.'

There were 12 men left. And the ship's cat. Billy's feet were swollen, 'my right foot a funny

Ted Jones, pictured here at 84, who saw the two halves of the ship lying on Barry Island beach – then sailed on her and had her sunk beneath him.

happened. The great old music hall comic Rob Wilton is remembered now for that one magical sentence... 'The day war broke out...'

The war which would bring so many deaths brought, ironically, a new lease of life for Cardiff and the other South Wales ports. Like Liverpool, another port in decline, they were in the best position to handle cargoes coming in from North America – vital food and raw materials – and it was like a return to the glory days as vessels waited days for a berth during the winter which would bring the blitz to South Wales. During those months of 1940-41 a third of the country's shipping business was handled by the South Wales ports. By the time they celebrated VE Day in Tiger

colour'. He began to take off the tips of his toes. When a Swedish vessel took them aboard he was carried piggy back. 'The only time the captain left the bridge was to operate on my right foot.'

Imagine it. Billy was taken to a cabin used as a hospital, then placed in a chair, his foot over a washbasin, before being held down by members of the crew.

'Peroxide alcohol was poured over my foot then the captain, using a scalpel, cut a piece away at a time. This was done over a couple of days. I could not be anaesthetised because of my condition.' Billy Andrews ended up in a hospital on the Faroe Islands where he went through skin grafting operations and then to Cardiff and the Hamadryad Hospital. But he went back to sea, his new ship part of the North African landing in 1943, so imminent its departure that no one gave Billy a medical examination.

But they did when he got back and tried to sign on again. He was sent to a surgery in James Street where Doctor Walker examined him. His verdict: 'Son, for you the war is over.' Billy would tell you years later that he was one of the lucky ones. Lucky? After having his feet hacked away in a ship's cabin? But that was life in those merchant ships sailing out of Cardiff.

Britain's merchant seamen never got the plaudits reserved for the other services. Yet they were as significant a factor in saving the country as the fabled Few, those fighter pilots so lauded over the years. Without them the country would have starved, been bereft of weapons and raw materials, and the price paid was colossal. By the end, more than 30,000 seamen had been lost, close to 2,500 ships sunk. The Merchant Seamen's Memorial in Cardiff Bay is a much needed nudge to the memory, reminding us that between the Battle of Britain and Hitler's invasion of Russia in June 1941, well over 60 ships were being sunk each month.

The skies over Kent, the thrust into the Soviet Union earned the big headlines. Just as today, one

At last they get the recognition they deserve: the memorial to the merchant seamen who died in two world wars and the Falklands is unveiled in 1997 at Cardiff Bay.

big aircrash with 200 killed is a sensation, while regular carnage on the roads is regarded with indifference. Right, let's get rid of the soapbox. And go on to perhaps the most exotic cargoes coming into Cardiff, arriving early in 1942 when 'the Yanks' were shipped in. Dockers like Mike Kennefick were not amused to be asked, by a GI whose notions of Britain had clearly been gathered from Hollywood, when he was going to put on his kilt. But the American invasion would have a profound effect on Tiger Bay, as we'll see later.

We've seen how the docks moved shipping in and out. But there was another, significant role to play and perhaps the saga of the *Tafelberg* sums it up best. Cardiff's eight dry docks were working round the clock to repair stricken ships but the *Talfelberg* was the biggest challenge. She was a 21,000 ton whaling factory steamer and either struck a mine laid by the Luftwaffe in the Bristol Channel or hit a rock. Whatever the reason, when she ended up on the beach at Barry Island she looked a lost cause. The vessel was broken completely in two, split right down amidships. But the two huge, twisted sections were temporarily fitted together and were then towed, slowly, tentatively, into the Channel Dry Dock. The parts were joined, an incredible job, and she was then reberthed in the Queen's Dock where heavy defensive guns were mounted.

Bert Jones, an ex-matelot from Cardiff, was a Royal Naval gun layer due to join the *Tafelberg*, renamed the *Empire Heritage,* but he was whipped on to another ship and so missed his place on the gun crew. But he never forgot the work carried out on the ship – so much skilled refitting on what they called the great stitchup – so complicated and successful a job, in fact, that James R. Main, works manager of the dry dock was later awarded the MBE for his supervision of the stitchup.

All in vain. The *Empire Heritage* joined the North Atlantic run where the U-Boat predators waited and was sunk on her first trip. Twenty years ago Ted Jones, then 84, remembered 'The Ship that Died Twice', and reckoned he was the only local survivor of the torpedo attack.

So the telegrams carrying the news every family dreaded came to Tiger Bay and the little streets of the Docks, but those families also felt the weight of war at home. Naturally the docks themselves were targeted – the German Air Force had detailed maps of the docks well before the outbreak of war. The first great raid was on the bitterly cold night of 2 January 1941 and it cost the lives of 165 people. Among them, almost 20 killed on Bute Street, including three Norwegian seamen who must have regarded Tiger Bay as a temporary haven after the risks at sea!

They were back at work the next day, business as usual. Just over Clarence Bridge, in Corporation Road, they were pulling 34 bodies out of the basement of Hollyman's Bakery – the basement, supposed to be bomb proof, was a shelter for local people. Bernard Moorcraft, later a stalwart of the Docks Conservative Club, remembered going to the door of the family butcher shop, ready to run across to the bakery.

'But there was so much going on, so many firebombs, my father told us to go back and try again.'

They went out during the next lull in the firestorm. Looked across the road. There was no bakery left. It was the biggest single death toll of the Cardiff blitz. Meanwhile, not far away in Neville Street, hit by a landmine, there was a happier ending. A rescue party dug for six hours guided by the sound of a childish voice singing, non-stop, God Save the King. They found a six-year-old boy crouched under the stairs. His father, he said, had been a miner 'and he told me that when men were trapped underground they would keep on singing and singing...'

But why God Save the King? It was, he said, 'The only tune I know.'

The Yanks Are Coming – But Billy the Seal Was First

WELL, we've already reflected that at one time there were 54 nationalities living together in Tiger Bay but a new dimension arrived with the Americans. The US Army still practised what amounted to apartheid and Cardiff saw, once more, race riots. What else, when black and white soldiers battled in local pubs solely on account of colour. Black GIs were ordered out of one cafe by a white officer – until the manager informed him we were not living in a 'back-of-the-bus society'. And on the corner of Bute Street and West Canal Wharf the signs went out: OFF LIMITS to US PERSONNEL.

But inevitably Tiger Bay became a magnet for many black GIs who found there a welcome from people who had formed a multi-racial – and at most times harmonious – society for three-quarters of a century. There were even GIs stationed in other parts of the country who went to Tiger Bay to spend their leave, among what they clearly considered their 'own people'.

And even when it was Off Limits they found a way in. Old residents remembered black GIs walking – or more likely stumbling – along the banks of the Taff to James Street so that they could enter the Bay from 'the other end', the end

The Yanks came to Cardiff wondering where the dockers' kilts were – and soon made themselves at home.

not so closely scrutinised by the Snowdrops, those Military Police whose random ferocity at times appalled local onlookers. As an impressionable small boy I personally saw one minuscule black GI being hauled along between two beefy Snowdrops while a third rattled his skull like a drum with the long, thick batons they flourished. Things could get even worse: a black driver who ignored the Off Limits sign and drove his Army truck down Bute Street was shot dead when he tried to escape from a patrol.

Deep South tactics had come to Tiger Bay...

Still, by the end of the war more than 70 Tiger Bay girls had become GI Brides and some still return for reunions. In 1982 the Lord Mayor, Coun Phil Dunleavy, hosted a civic reception for them in Cardiff Castle. So what did they think of the city they'd left.

'When I was a kid,' said Mrs Jean Deberry, who'd swapped Loudoun Square for Washington DC, 'we had a park but now all I see are skyscrapers.' She meant the tower block flats so disastrously erected where the square had been. At least, she added, 'They've kept St Mary's Church. I hope they'll never knock that down.' Maybe those people who hadn't seen the Bay for more than 20 years had a clearer perspective of what had happened to it than the rest of us.

There could have been more of those brides coming home – but some of those GIs who so loved Tiger Bay, who might have been husbands, would never return. In 1944 they were being prepared for the invasion of Europe, and Cardiff and the other ports were handling the torrent of supplies coming across the Atlantic. It really was a torrent: almost four fifths of all supplies to the US forces in Britain came through locally and Cardiff's docks were actually taken over by the Americans with a US Port Commander in charge, American troops working alongside the overstretched Cardiff dockers.

Mike Kennefick remembered the land around the Alexandra Dock crammed with guns and

But for many the journey to their real homes was made in a coffin after the war.

tanks. Dockers had already been astonished at the huge locomotives brought in to replace clapped-out railway stock and now, at first hand, they were witnessing the apparently limitless power of the United States at war. Some 48 hours before D Day, 6 June, the amazing convoy bound for the French beaches sailed out of Cardiff and down the Bristol Channel. Another Cardiff connection – the GIs who unloaded crucial cargoes in France had been trained in the docks.

After the war General Dwight D. Eisenhower, 'Ike' to all, sent a message to the men of the South Wales ports, thanking them 'for your contribution

Cardiff's Lord Mayor Alderman R.G. Robinson, presents a Welsh flag to the skipper of the SS Lawrence Victory before the ship left Cardiff docks with the remains of 4,383 American airmen.

to victory and the cooperation you gave to the United States forces.' No doubt about it, Cardiff docks – oh, all right, and Newport and Penarth – had played a vital part in the greatest invasion ever mounted. What a difference almost 40 years later when another invasion fleet sailed. When sending a task force to the South Atlantic to reclaim the Falklands, Britain had to charter foreign merchant ships for the support fleet. A reflection on the way the docks had declined, the way in which our shipping had shrunk.

The saddest symbolic ending for many docks people came when Neale and West sailed their trawlers out of Cardiff for the last time. They had never been glamorous ships, never spelled out romance or conjured up visions of far-off places. But they did bring one glorious character to Cardiff along with the fish – and there's even a statue of him, or rather her, to remind us of the company's great days.

But (again) to begin at the beginning…

Joshua Neale and Henry West began business together as fish merchants in Custom House Street, then the city's Covent Garden and Billingsgate combined. Being as optimistic as most of the Docksmen congregating in Cardiff they decided to catch their own fish and so, in 1888, they moved to the West Dock and, with a single trawler, started a great local tradition. That was the year when Cardiff shipped out seven million tons of coal and the Welsh sailing ship *Merioneth* set a new record for a trip to far-off California, rounding the Horn to reach San Francisco in 96 days.

The docks, then, were clearly on the move and Joshua and Henry decided to move with them. By 1906 they owned a fleet of 19 ships and many a lad from the Bay and the Docks and Grangetown started his seagoing career aboard a Neale and West trawler. Hard, hard work and it took hard men to do it.

And this glorious character connected with them?

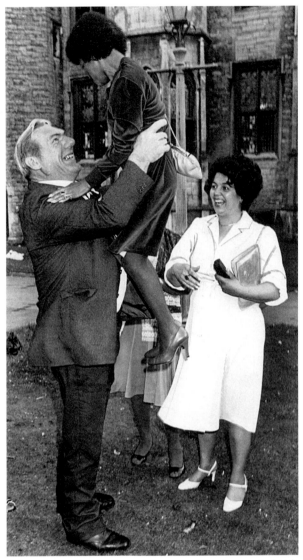

A happier ending to the war for some GIs who married girls from the Bay. And here's Viv Brook welcoming Mrs Rita McMillen Logan home for a visit along with 40 other GI brides. Mrs Valerie Johnson waits her turn.

Well, in 1912, a Neale and West trawler hauled in its nets to find, among the cod, a young seal. They brought him back into port and he took up residence – well let Frank Hennessy, the local minstrel tell us:

'He lived in a pond in Victoria Park, where they fed him on kippers an' flagons of Dark.'

During the 1920s when the River Ely overflowed, Victoria Park was flooded and Billy,

Mrs Betty Ellul, left, of Loudoun Square, welcomes home her GI bride sister Mrs Jean De Berry who, like the others, was glad to see that at least St Mary's Church was still there.

He lived in a pond in Victoria Park... and in 1997 they unveiled a statue of Billy the Seal, Cardiff's favourite fish-gobbler.

so legend says, decided it was an opportunity to go back and have a look around the docks. So out he swam to board a passing tramcar, hopping off near a pub where he turned up with a kipper in his flipper. But he had not only swum from the park. He had swum into local folklore, becoming, in the process, one of Cardiff's most famous and best-loved citizens.

He lived on in the pond, one of the city's star attractions, and died in 1939, yes, the Year War Broke Out.

Now I have to interject a personal note. For long after Billy's death Georgie Parsons, an old friend who has since joined Billy in some celestial park, told me that in 1939 he was on the dole while 'doing a bit of an 'obble' at the Museum in Cardiff's civic centre.

'Me and Johnny Houlston (a celebrated Cardiff boxer) was digging a sort of steel vault where they'd put their treasures in if war broke out when this chap emerges from the Museum.' Would George and Johnny, this chap wondered, be prepared to dig a grave for a small remuneration. After discovering that a small remuneration wasn't a little furry animal from South America, the pair agreed.

Who for? George enquired. For Billy the Seal, the Museum chap whispered. Our fish-gulping hero had been found dead when his keeper arrived with the breakfast bloater. George and Johnny dug the grave behind the Museum into which he was lowered. Job done, they thought. But no.

'All of a sudden this lady in a white coat appears. She wants to empty it in with Billy. And in this box, George recalled, were 'about six thousand little insects... 'orrible little things, they were.'

In they went and Billy was covered up. Six weeks later, for another small remuneration, George and Johnny dug up Billy the Seal. The 'orrible little things had done their job well. Only a skeleton remained. 'Picked clean.' George recalled with awe.

End of story? Not quite. For Billy's skeleton finally surfaced, if that's the word, during renovations at the Museum and an examination showed that from 1912 to 1939 Billy had conned the city. For He was really a She. So if for nothing else, although there is plenty, Neale and West should always be remembered for Billy – let's face it, no one will ever call him/her Millie. Sadly the last trawlers sailed out of Cardiff and into history in 1956 and Cardiff for the first time in centuries was no longer a fishing port, no longer would 'the lads off the trawlers' descend on the pubs of Tiger Bay after three weeks of seagoing hell.

Summer on the Costa Del Canal

THE end of Neale and West, the end of Billy the Seal. So many endings in those docks. But few so sad as that which came in December 1951. The old Glamorganshire Canal had been dead for years, only the sea lock kept in use. But on that December day Cardiff saw the final nail hammered into the coffin: on that day the sand dredger *Catherine Ethel* crashed into the inner lock gates and out rushed the waters as though a gigantic plug had been pulled. The Glamorganshire Canal was emptied forever, 153 years after the great day of its opening.

And now it was a day of mourning for the boys of the Bay and the lads from the Docks.

Why mourn an old canal which had long outlived its use? Ah, but it hadn't. And once more I have to declare an interest. For like those boys from the Bay, the lads from the Docks, the canal

The canal feeder running across Bute Street, the side of the Custom House to the left.

The canal and the James Street swing bridge.

The Costa de Docks – water sports in the sea lock before World War One.

had been part of my life. During the long summer holidays when all the world was warm and the skies eternally blue (they always were, you know) the canal was our watery wonderland while the sand piled high on the bank offered beaches as seductive as any found in Bali and a lot cheaper to get to than Barry Island. No sparkling sea along the Costa del Sol could ever be as inviting as the black, oil-slicked water of the Canal. And no

And on the swing bridge itself – with kids sitting there looking down the canal.

modern mother would allow her little darlings within a mile of the place as it was in those dreamy days. Imagine their feelings as their little ones dived off the side of the old dredgers, maybe the famous Delorain, into the unknown, to grope on the bottom among discarded junk and leg-trapping detritus. Even then, some things were best kept from mothers.

Who cared? Into the water, then out to sprawl on the sand in the sun, plucking up courage to climb the mast, then swallow dive (we wished) some 30 feet. From Kingsway down, the canal and the River Taff were swimming pools, lidos for generations of Cardiff kids, but the Docks end with those dredgers came first.

And of course, some plunged in, never to resurface. That's when an old dockland custom would be used. Bread or straw was thrown on to the water and where it floated, there you could be sure, you'd find the corpse. Docks historian Bill Barrett once fondly recalled a couple of characters renowned for their life saving activities. When the *South Wales Echo* added up their scores we found them both over the 90 mark. The two heroes were instantly the focus of all attention. After the article celebrating their exploits appeared they took to patrolling the canal banks with all the vigilance of old time revenue officers, both seeking a century.

'Any splash of water,' said Bill, 'would see one of them come running, hopeful of adding to the tally.' But after the *Echo's* ominous count everyone was so careful that the figures remained static all through the summer, and autumn, with the canal too cold for swimming, found them disappointed men.

But besides being a playground, the canal

Mrs Margaret Watkins, landlady of the Bridge Hotel on Bute Street, looks anxiously down at her sons Glyn and Vivian as they play alongside the canal where so many had drowned.

offered a home for the city's own – well, call them water gypsies. People lived in houseboats moored to the banks, cooking on primus stoves, their nights lit only by hurricane lamps. Many of the 'houses' were old lifeboats bought for as little as a pound, then rowed around to settle in shallows leading up from an old ballast beach on the west side of the canal. Corrugated iron and timber was tarred over to provide a weather-defying top. The boat people were accepted and they knew it when the council finally put in a standpipe after housebound neighbours got fed up with providing water every day.

Perhaps the most famous – or even infamous – of Cardiff's boat people was a gent rejoicing in

the name of Donkey James. He kept his donkey in a lean-to attached to the boat, complete with a little cart which was sometimes a golden coach for Docks' kids. Donkey's wife collected firewood which she sold to shops while Donkey trotted off to one of the local pubs. Bill Barrett recalled he'd leave the donkey and cart outside the Big Windsor – later a renowned gourmet restaurant – while he downed a couple of pints. One night some jokers unhitched the cart and pushed the shafts through nearby railings. Then they led the donkey round to the other side of the railings, and rehitched.

When Donkey emerged from the pub he took one look, then observed 'It's enough to make a man sign the pledge.' He didn't, of course, and in

The end of the watery road down from Merthyr: the lock gates.

And here's a little vessel going in about a century earlier.

But it all ended when the sand dredger Catherine Ethel *crashed into the inner gates in December 1951 and emptied the sea lock of the Glamorganshire Canal. Here's the culprit pictured earlier with the Norwegian Church in the background.*

time, like so much else and so many others around the docks and Tiger Bay, he simply faded away with the houseboats.

No, it wasn't the sort of housing standard we'd approve of today. But those saucy little boats added a spicy flavour to the docks in days when regattas were held in front of the dock gates, when the canal was the city's biggest street. And when it was emptied we discovered that it had also come pretty close to being the city's biggest rubbish dump, as well. They ambled up from the Bay and the Docks to look down on the emptiness and there was a vista of rusted old bike frames, prams and pushchairs, so much detritus that the *Echo* reported that treasure-seekers were flocking

to the trove in search of rumoured riches. There were rumours in plenty – of safes being found beneath the mud, of money boxes still stuffed, of jewellery. But really, the greatest treasure lost was that water, the playground, the Costa del Docks. No leisure centre pool, no matter how lavishly equipped, can ever bring the joys of that canal.

Well, we've had the houseboats. So what about the hospital boat? Here, while gently reminiscing, we come to another legendary fragment of docks' history – the *Hamadryad*. If only... if only. If only Cardiff had had the sense to keep her as Portsmouth kept Nelson's *Victory*, what an attraction it – sorry, *she* would have been.

The photograph below decks towards the end

They'd already started filling in the lower reaches, and here's the section behind Custom House Street before running under the bridge by the Custom House itself.

of the 19th century looks like the sick bay aboard HMS *Victory* the day after Trafalgar. Stuffed with old seadogs who heard Horatio whisper 'Kiss me Hardy.' Close, but not quite. Although this 1,000 ton, 21-gun frigate was built as a direct result of Trafalgar she never fired a shot in anger. Instead she ended up in Cardiff docks and her name is now part of folklore – and still owned by the hospital built 'ashore'.

She was launched in 1823 just in case there was a rematch with the French but in spite of the (then) massive £24,683 she cost she never fired one of her 46 guns in anger. She was in time for the Crimea and the Charge of the Light Brigade but she stayed in Devonport dockyard in 1854 while other, newer vessels went to war. In effect,

she was under sentence of death. But the reprieve came when, instead of being broken up, she came to Cardiff in 1866 as a life-saver instead of potential life-taker. In November that year she opened as a hospital for seamen, moored on a little muddy peninsula between the Taff and the sea lock of the Glamorganshire Canal.

On 1 November that year the *Cardiff Times* reported: 'The fitting up has been effected with great care and regard for the comfort of the patients, as well as the prevention of the spread of infectious disorders.'

Infectious disorders? Well, knowing old sailors, knowing Tiger Bay, it's as well not to ask, given that in those Victorian times even uncovered piano legs were regarded as inflammatory – or so

But children still played on the canal banks.

we're told. By the 1880s 500 in-patients and ten times that many out-patients were stepping – or being carried – aboard the *Hamadryad* each year. You can imagine the crack, the tall tales down below as these old salts got together. The dawn must have come up like thunder a dozen times a day as they droned on about that Road to Mandalay. (Think Uncle Albert in *Only Fools and Horses*).

This unique hospital was financed by the employers of the men who used it. Shipping companies paid 2s for every 100 tons of shipping entering the port and there were also considerable sums donated by the tycoons of the time, the Corys and the Seagars. But as the docks grew so did the little streets on land around the ship and it

was clear that it would have to be replaced. After all, there were only 60 bunks and room had to be found for doctor, matron and their staffs as well. So in 1896, it was decided to build a Royal Seamen's Hospital for men of all nations.

What better way, cried the town's elders, to celebrate Queen Victoria's Diamond Jubilee the following year. Land for the ambitious new project was donated by the Marques of Bute and the Taff Vale Railway and in 1905, the year (I must repeat) when Wales beat the first mighty All Blacks, a splendid new brick building was opened. It is still operational at the time of writing but could eventually be amalgamated with one of the bigger hospitals planned for Cardiff.

But what of the original *Hamadryad*? Or

And on the banks of the Taff estuary in the early 1950s.

rather, the third ship of that name – the first was the Spanish frigate *Ninfa*, captured in 1797 as she was unloading treasure from Cuba on to the fishing boats off Cadiz (where Drake had earlier 'singed the King of Spain's beard'). Ninfa is Spanish for nymph, but there was already a ship of the line with that name, so the frigate was renamed *Hamadryad*, or wood nymph. The second *Hamadryad*? She survives simply as a name. But we know the sad end for the third, *our Hamadryad*. The old war-horse, or maybe seahorse, went to that nautical death she'd escaped so many years earlier. In 1905 (the year Wales beat...) she was sold and towed to Bideford where she was broken up after decades of healing broken bodies.

By one of those odd quirks which seem to be endemic when you speak of the Docks and Tiger Bay, another ancient frigate went to her death in that same year. Cardiff seems to have been a sort of elephants' graveyard for ships, if you can untangle the metaphor. She was the *Havannah*, another frigate built during the Napoleonic Wars. This 42-gun vessel was launched in 1811 and her history is a little more exotic than that of the old *Hamadryad*. For the *Havannah* was one of the men-o-war which escorted the defeated Napoleon to exile on St Helena in 1815 – the year, incidentally, in which Shaka, 'The Napoleon of Africa', began the foundation of the Zulu empire. To digress: 64 years on, Cetawayo, a successor King of the Zulus, would see his men smash British troops at Isandhlwana, the first great victory by Africans over white colonists. A couple of days later 4,000 Zulus were driven back at Rorke's Drift by 140 British soldiers, thus giving

The Hamadryad *Hospital, brought to Cardiff in 1866 and berthed in the East Dock.*

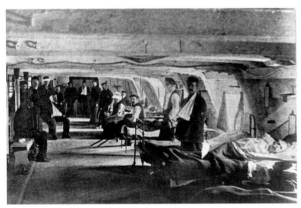

Some of the first patients aboard her looking like survivors of Trafalgar.

The Hamadryad's *figurehead was moved to the hospital built in 1902 and kept in the waiting room there. Nurse Mary Willis is dwarfed by the giant head in 1971.*

Michael Caine his big break almost a century later in the film *Zulu*, celebrating that battle. The heroes, who earned 11 VC's, included Welshmen. In the movie one was played by Ivor Emmanuel who sang *Men of Harlech* as the Zulu horde advanced. 'Stop singing, Ivor boy,' someone shouted. 'Then perhaps they'll stop throwing spears at us.'

No, I made that up. So let's get back to the *Havannah*.

In 1860 she was regarded as just another old hulk – but yet again, as in the case of the *Hamadryad*, there was a reprieve. Instead of being broken up she came to Cardiff, on loan from the Admiralty to the Dickensian-named Industrial and Ragged School Committee, a typical body of Victorian philanthropists. Life on the streets hadn't changed much since Dickens published Oliver Twist 22 years before and the spectre of Fagin and his band of boy brigands still hung heavy. Anything to prevent new little Olivers, destitute young lads, from turning to crime. Hence the ragged school movement designed to 'make better provision for the care and education of vagrant, destitute and disorderly children.'

By the 1880s there were 80 boys aboard the *Havannah*, moored near the East Dock before moving to a specially carved 'dock' above Penarth Road Bridge. They were taught knotting, reefing, splicing, sail-making, rowing and, in anticipation of future life at sea, cutlass drill. But by 1888 the town's *Havannah* Committee called the vessel 'a decaying hulk… age and weather have rendered her top-sides too rotten to be made waterproof by

Cardiff's other 'warship', the Havannah. *She was among the ships escorting Napoleon into exile on St Helena in 1815 and came to the East Dock in 1860 before being turned into a 'Ragged School'.*

caulking.' No wonder the town council's medical officer reported a year later that 'It would be unwise to incur any considerable expenses in endeavouring to improve the condition of this ship.'

It sounds almost like a bigger version of Donkey James' houseboat. But the boys stayed aboard and in 1905, the year when Cardiff became a city, the *Havannah* was sold to a Mr Harry Norris. After breaking up the old frigate he presented two of her guns to the Cardiff Corporation and they were placed in Roath Park. But when a bigger war than Napoleon or Wellington had ever dreamed of began in 1914 they were taken away for scrap metal. It's intriguing to wonder whether part of that old Ragged School was ever used in the awful killing fields of the Somme. Or whether any of its old boys were there at Jutland or even perhaps on HMS Cardiff as she led the surrendered German fleet to Scapa Flow.

Odd to think that today's HMS Cardiff probably packs as much devastating firepower as that entire German fleet. But that's progress. Or maybe not.

Tiger Bay: Where Fiction is Stranger Than Fact

'TO SAILORMEN *the world over Tiger Bay recalls that grimy but strangely fascinating area of the docks at Cardiff where ships from all the Seven Seas tie up and disgorge their diverse cargoes and, for a brief time, their stranger crews. Here amid the drab streets still lingers something of the spirit of adventure and even of romance. Dark faces peer from darker doorways, raucous music blares from tiny cafes, countless feet patter by, some with stealthy tread, others in hurried agitation, feet that have known the waterfront of many distant ports.'*

How about that then? But don't blame me. That is the cover blurb for a book called *Once In Tiger Bay* by J.M. Walsh, published in 1947. Sax Rohmer had given us dirty doings in Limehouse with Fu Manchu, and Edgar Wallace frequently used the London docks as the obvious choice for his slant-eyed Mastermind's lair. Tiger Bay clearly offered as much atmosphere, mystery and threatening Orientals etc. and J.M. Walsh cashed in. He wrote two other thrillers about the place, featuring a police inspector called John Maurey as hero, a sort of Viv Brook without the neck. They were *Return to Tiger Bay* and *King of Tiger Bay*. Here's a sample of Maurey's thoughts on accession to the Throne down the Bay…

'In the past more than one man has had ambitions to make himself King of Tiger Bay. But it never really worked. Usually it's ended in a quiet little funeral or in someone being sent to the Awful Place.'

Well, tell that to Bob Downey. But the description the Awful Place is pure Edgar Wallace. In fact, he used that term to describe Dartmoor. As far as J.M. Walsh was concerned – let's quote again – 'Tiger Bay was the place where one was more likely to meet with adventure than any other spot in Britain.' You don't believe him? Hang on.

'Here is one of those meeting places of the Seven Seas and the weather-beaten men who sail them, and of the strange men and women of the underworld who follow sailormen in every port.'

I know nothing about J.M. Walsh but I wonder whether he ever actually visited Tiger Bay. For listen to a mountainous black man talking to a white visitor in *Once In Tiger Bay*: The white man is alone.

'Plenty folks would have been scared,' the Negro concluded. 'Yes Sah. Specially white folk. They don't come down here much by day, let alone by night.'

Consider the fact that there were 'plenty folks' who were white actually living down the Bay and here you have a classic example of the demonisation of the Bay: and remember, when those books were written the 'thriller' was the equivalent of the hour-long cop show on today's TV. So anyone reading J.M. Walsh must have believed that Tiger Bay was packed with villains rejoicing in such names as Emplicado, Vitongo, Spazzare, while there was a real low-life called Farina who didn't so much walk as 'sidle unobtrusively out of the deep purple darkness' into, where else, Suey Lim's very dubious establishment.

Why no nasties named Jones or Evans or even Downey? Especially when one evildoer is introduced as, 'a celebrated character of the underworld,' who puts up with the name Whistling Dick.

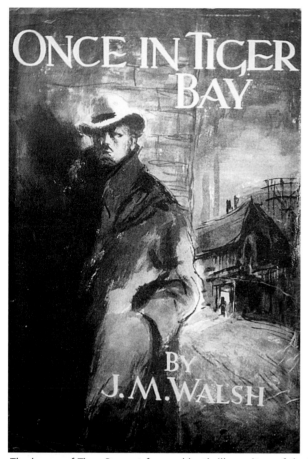

The image of Tiger Bay put forward by thriller writers of the 1940s. The covers of 'Bay books' by J.M. Walsh.

And the reason for the above is to introduce you, hopefully, to Tiger Bay and the Docks in fiction, film and television. Walsh was a bit of a pioneer but he served up Tiger Bay as myth, rather than reality. But that's what fiction's all about and it's astonishing that more has not been made of that place where, according to J. M. Walsh, dark faces peered from even darker doorways.

That was written in the 1940s. The fictional approach to Tiger Bay hadn't changed much even by the 1960s. Here's a police inspector (not Maurey) helping out a visitor.

'It's down by the docks, in the district you probably know as Tiger bay.'

'Oh yes,' I said. 'Where Shirley Bassey comes from.'

'No,' he said. 'She comes from Splott... not Tiger Bay at all. That's just newspaper talk.'

Once more, Tiger Bay is dangerous, as in all fiction. The police, we're told, steer clear of it. 'My officers have instructions, in fact, to approach the place only in pairs. Lascars, there are. And Maltese from the ships. And the so-called whites are the worst of the lot.'

That was taken from *It Won't Get you Anywhere*, by Desmond Skirrow and out of the windows of his Bute Street come animal sounds... a straight human scream... a giggle and a a snort – 'That's how little Taffies are born.' Still, as one of Skirrow's villains was called Tonypandy Williams the good news was that all the nasties didn't have names ending in O.

John Williams, an author who captured the spirit of the Bay, in familiar surroundings.

Paul Robeson, always remembered by the people of the Bay for Sanders of the River, *the film for which they provided some of the extras.*

Years later the legend, if only partly, lived on. Here's another Cardiff docks copper, David Brade, talking about his patch in the nineties:

'*This was his realm, was still his realm, more or less. By night it kept a few murky traces of how it had always been – the girls, the gangs, the violence. And by day... By day, it looked transfigured. It had a marina now, and a lot of bright, new, dinky-scale, cement-brick housing. Old warehouses had been gutted with imagination and turned into apartment blocks...*'

From his book *Forget It*, by David Craig, who, usually as Bill James, is one of Britain's most celebrated writers of crime fiction. Craig (confusingly his real

name is Jim Tucker, a former journalist and university lecturer), knows the docks old and new and you'll find no Fu Manchus gliding down his Bute Street.

Nor is that Master of Evil in *Fire in the Bay*, a fictional look at life between the wars in Tiger Bay by Tom Davies. Here we have a prostitute finding fame as a singer, an idealistic minister who feels impelled to do a sort of missionary work among the natives, and a shipowner with Fascist leanings. All against the background of those riots and racial tensions with a bit of mysticism thrown in.

And then John Williams came along with *Five Pubs, Two Bars and a Nightclub* to offer a truly authentic

Hayley Mills, young star of the film Tiger Bay, arrives in Cardiff for the world premiere with parents John and Mary in March 1959.

picture of the Bay and its life in fiction. That was followed by *Cardiff Dead* – title from the Hennessy song, 'I'm Cardiff born and Cardiff bred, And when I dies I'll be Cardiff dead.' Williams gives us a tremendous tale set against the 'new' Cardiff, a city with no room for the old ways. And while J.M. Walsh and Skirrow seem to have written about the Bay only through second hand experience and hearsay, Williams writes as one born in the Bay although his childhood was spent in one of Cardiff's classiest neighbourhoods, Cyncoed. If you want to sense what life in this changing corner of Cardiff is all about, John Williams' fiction will give you as good an idea as any.

But Williams' finest work so far – and probably the catalyst for his involvement with the Bay – is *Bloody Valentine*, an account of the murder of the prostitute Lynette White on St Valentine's Day, 1988. It dramatically underlines the fact that although Shanghai Walsh and Larry the Maltese might be long gone, the pimps, the villains and the prostitutes still find space in Tiger Bay – or Butetown to be politically correct.

Of course, the most monumental novel about Cardiff's docks and Dockland came from Jack Jones whose *River Out of Eden* appeared in 1951. This old-fashioned 'family saga' traces the history of what we might call one of those Docksmen, an Irish immigrant who made it to the top. It's the story of the growth of the docks and of Cardiff and the Bute dynasty as well: in today's jargon, 'faction', a handy way to study the history of the city over the century ending in the 1940s.

And inevitably, the Bay could hardly avoid being featured on film. It was called – equally inevitably - *Tiger Bay* and told the story of a young seamen being hunted for a murder although, as he was played by handsome Horst Bucholtz, it was, of course, accidental death. In those days matinee idols couldn't be *real* murderers. He was sheltered by a Tomboyish girl played by 12-year-old Hayley Mills, daughter of John, who was another

fictional Cardiff copper. The people of the Bay provided extras – as they had done when Paul Robeson made *Sanders of the River* in the 1930s – and it still causes a nostalgic stir when shown on late night television. It's intriguing, too, for the glimpses of the bygone city it gives us – the last chance to see some of those streets for at the time it was made Tiger Bay, old Tiger Bay, was under sentence of death with redevelopment approaching.

Well, on 23 March 1959, it was given its world premiere in Cardiff's Gaumont Theatre (gone with so much else) and as the *Western Mail* announced, 'All the glamour and glitter of a West End premiere came to Cardiff last night.' Crowds packed Queen Street 'and surged forward when the stars arrived.' A fabulous night, wrote the *Echo* film critic, and although he hated to take an I-told-you-so attitude the film proved 'that the argument about Tiger Bay being shown as a hotbed of everything evil was so much hot air.'

The argument? Ah yes, powerful voices had been raised in protest at the naming of the film. No less a person than the future Prime Minister James Callaghan, the local MP, tried to get the name changed. It was, he said, a libel on the area and the impression of Tiger Bay given in the film was completely untrue. Cardiff councillors wondered why the city should spend money advertising its civic beauty 'while allowing a film to be made with this title that is harmful to Cardiff.' Meanwhile, three weeks before the premiere the city's venerable Town Clerk, S. Tapper Jones, speaking at a public enquiry into the proposed compulsory purchase of land in the area observed: 'Such films as *Tiger Bay* grossly misrepresent what you will find when you visit the area.'

Then, in the spirit of censors everywhere who condemn without reading the book, watching the play or actually seeing the film – he hadn't – he thundered that it was 'a gross misrepresentation.' To see it now is to wonder what all the fuss was

Then in 1997 they brought Tiger Bay *to television, all the glitz of Hollywood coming to the little streets.*

But for actors Robert Gwilym and Mike Hayward (seen here in the Bay's only remaining boatyard, fictional, naturally) there were no long term contracts as in Coronation Street. Tiger Bay *finished after one series.*

about. We had to wait almost 40 years to see the cameras rolling once again around Bute Street and the docks and, despite the criticisms of *that* film, this Welsh TV soap was also called *Tiger Bay*.

The first 30-minute episode in July 1997, introduced us to a Yuppie solicitor and his go-for-it young wife, the chopsy woman boss of a taxi company and the mandatory wise-cracking cabbie, a murderer fresh out of prison and a mother driven to suicide. All this was followed by the fire-bombing of an Asian businessman's car by a gang of black youths and, among other oddities, a 16-year-old girl seducing a bloke twice her age.

Yes, there were Welsh actors and Welsh accents as promised, But long before that first episode was screened there were misgivings among the real people of the Bay. Writers in the community who thought they'd be involved in devising story lines were disappointed and, after seeing the first scripts threatened 'direct action'. Why? Because those 'negative' scripts showed, besides the fire-

bombing of the car, incest between a brother and sister and 'conflict between members of the long-established Butetown community and incomers who have moved to new developments like Atlantic Wharf. In reality there is little contact between the two communities.'

Some five million viewers watched on that first night, the critics were kind and things looked good. But only three million switched on for the final episode of the first series in September. And that was the last Cardiff saw of Jodie and Roy, Sonny and Gary, Bernie and Charlie. Now if they had set it all in the 1920s and 1930s with Bob Downey and Shanghai Walsh and Father Purveau...

A Tiger Bay Welcome for a Turbulent Priest

AND talking of Father Purveau – let's not forget that religion has always been as much a part of the Bay as any of the, shall we say more publicised aspects. We've already chronicled the way in which the twin towers of St Mary's were finally financed to give Tiger Bay its most enduring landmark. But there was another building which was perhaps as beloved a symbol of religion in the Bay.

They built the Norwegian Church in 1868 and for over a century it stood at the entrance to the West Dock, its white walls and 'witch-hat' spire so

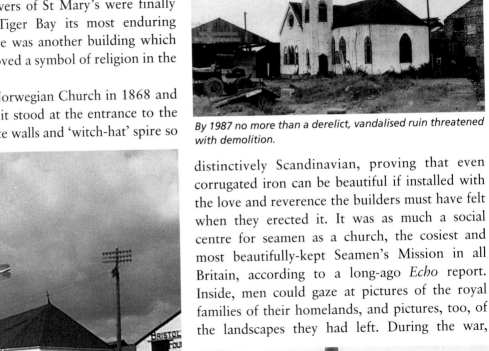

By 1987 no more than a derelict, vandalised ruin threatened with demolition.

distinctively Scandinavian, proving that even corrugated iron can be beautiful if installed with the love and reverence the builders must have felt when they erected it. It was as much a social centre for seamen as a church, the cosiest and most beautifully-kept Seamen's Mission in all Britain, according to a long-ago *Echo* report. Inside, men could gaze at pictures of the royal families of their homelands, and pictures, too, of the landscapes they had left. During the war,

The Norwegian Church at the end of the 1960s, approaching its own end.

But at last, a new lease of life when it's rebuilt as part of the new Bay, now used for exhibitions and entertainments.

when exiled from home, it was more of a link than ever with those northern lands.

Sadly, as the docks declined, as shipping slumped, so did the church. In 1984 there was a break-in and sundry items were removed. Including the pulpit. Technically a theft but, as I wrote at the time, 'But I am 100 per cent in favour of the felon (or felons). They committed their 'crime' because to leave the furnishings where they were would have meant their inevitable destruction.' It had last been used in 1970 for centenary celebrations (delayed?) and since then had gradually slipped towards slumdom. Inside at the time the pulpit was taken you found a drawing of a horned and bearded head above the legend SATANISM with an upside-down crucifix painted on to the wall. Ominous, indeed. There seemed no future for the church built originally as a haven for seamen bringing in timber for pit props from their Scandinavian forests.

In 1987, in fact, it was threatened with demolition but was saved when the Norwegian Church Preservation Trust was formed. The building was dismantled until, five years later, Princess Martha Louise of Norway officially reopened the rebuilt church not far from its original position. More than £200,000 had been raised in Britain and in Norway to ensure that it could begin its new life as a cultural centre. As the Princess approached the church she was greeted by people who had once worshipped there, wearing national costume. And with her was Mrs Felicity Dahl, the president of the trust and widow of children's author supreme, Roald Dahl. He had been baptised in the church in 1916 and a gallery room in honour of his life and work is part of the new centre, still one of the most distinctive buildings in all of Dockland.

Well, the Scandinavians were among the earliest visitors to our city – remember those Vikings cruising up the Taff? But the Greeks had come early to Cardiff as well. And in 1906 the Greek communities of Cardiff, Barry and Newport built their Orthodox Church in the Bay, the gorgeous interior at odds with the drabness outside.

And also as a memorial for the celebrated children's author Roald Dahl, born in Cardiff, christened in the church.

And of course, there are the mosques. The Noor el Islam Mosque arrived in 1947, minarets and characteristic dome bringing images out of the Arabian Nights to Tiger Bay. It was replaced in 1984 by a £400,000 building which was destined to be the centre of worship for the 7,000-strong Moslem community in Cardiff. It hadn't been easy. Donations from some Arab governments failed to materialise although the city's Moslem leaders had toured Arab states and had received promises of aid. It took a £50,000 donation from a Yemeni businessman to rescue the project but now Cardiff's only purpose-built mosque on dear old Alice Street is a glorious addition to the new Bay, its dome and minaret a new and vivid Tiger Bay landmark. Incidentally, in 1968 the foundation stone for the Islamic Centre for Wales was laid in Tiger Bay. And the man who laid it? Our old friend the Muslim boxer, Sheik Said Hassan.

Sadder news, though, for St Stephen's Church in Mount Stuart Square, no longer in use.

Of course there were other churches and chapels. Yet another old hulk, HMS *Thisbe*, was moored in the East Dock in 1860, becoming, in time, the Gospel Ship and Mission to seamen. Loudoun Square had its Methodist Mission and there were chapels and churches in Bute street and Mount Stuart Square. And in the 1840s the Irish immigrants from Newtown attended Mass in a

house on Bute Street until neighbouring Bute Terrace became home for Cardiff's first Roman Catholic Church.

It's worth pausing to consider those Roman Catholics. In a way they were part of the docks and Tiger Bay, but, well… not quite. Newtown – 'Little Ireland' – was built on land east of Bute Street and it got its name because it was here that the Irish flocking into Cardiff to escape the Famine were herded. Irish Catholic muscle helped build the great docks and the Marquess of Bute of the time is supposed to have prayed for forgiveness in St John's Church for bringing 'boatloads of papists' to Wales. Ironically, the Butes later became one of Britain's most prominent Catholic families.

Nothing but hope in the future at the dedication in 1912.

These asylum-seekers of their day were herded into what was no more than a ghetto. Conditions were scarcely better than those they had left behind. They existed in tiny houses, often flooded by sewage, and the death toll was horrendous during the cholera and typhoid epidemics of mid-Victorian Cardiff. But they survived, the women worked unloading potato ships on the docks as their children became dockers and in time, lawyers, lecturers, and numbered even Lord Mayors of the city among them.

And of course, the most famous son of all was Peerless Jim Driscoll, who died in 1925 and who went to his grave, we remind you, mourned by 100,000 fellow citizens. There's a statue of Jim at the 'town end' of Bute Street but not much else to

Old churches die. New mosques rise. Here is the Noor el Islam Mosque on Peel Street before demolition in the early 1960s.

But in 1968 the foundation stone of a new Mosque is laid – the ceremony performed by that former boxer Sheik Said Hassan.

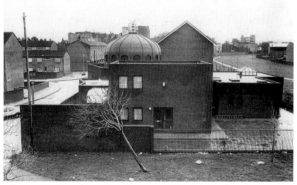

The new Mosque at Alice Street, the path of the old Glamorganshire Canal to the right.

With the former Prime Minister (and local MP) James Callaghan at the official opening in 1984 of the new Mosque at Alice Street

A service in the Greek Orthodox Church built in 1906 close to St Mary's. This was in 1959.

Three photographs of Bay Muslims.

remind you of Little Ireland which, like Tiger Bay, is no more. To stay in context: Requiescat in Pace.

Another priest, a famous, even legendary priest came to the Bay. And this, perhaps, was the most memorable visit of all, and one of the most memorable days in Tiger Bay history – for this visit was reported worldwide.

Father Trevor Huddlestone had become a dedicated – and feared – enemy of Apartheid during the 12 years he ministered in South Africa. But he incensed the government of that country more than ever when, in his book *Naught For Your Comfort*, he wrote of the appalling black slums where he had worked. Father Huddlestones's views were read around the globe – the South African government decided to deflect the heat. So the challenge came from the country's External Affairs Minister, Eric Louw.

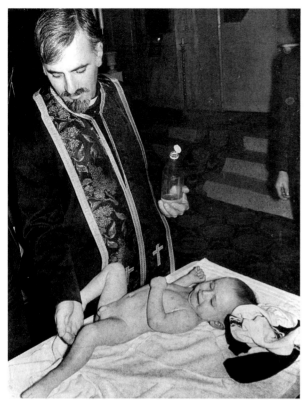

And in 1970 the Revd S. Dessillas anoints the body of 13-month-old Alexis Morgan with ceremonial oil before his christening.

Time for a cuppa and a discussion about the state of the Bay with the locals.

'The slums of Cardiff's Butetown are worse than anything in South Africa. Go and investigate them.'

Trevor Huddlestone did. And on a grey March day in 1957 he came to Tiger Bay. He began in Loudoun Square and ended his tour, after a stop in a Bay club run by a West African, patronised by black and white, by saying that judged by civilised standards Butetown was, yes was a slum. 'But compared with South Africa's black slums it is a paradise.'

The people of the Bay welcomed this tall, close-cropped priest as he walked through the Square and Peel Street and Sophia Street. He watched the children, black, white and brown learning together, playing together, and shook his head. 'If only we could have this in South Africa… what a wonderful community.' Butetown, he enthused,

was a marvellous example of the way in which people of different races could live happily together. When he went into St Mary's School he was astonished – and delighted – to find children of 18 different races studying together. 'You must keep this school going,' he told the vicar, Father B.M. Oman. And then: 'Oh, how I wish it could be so in South Africa. What a big, happy family. What a wonderful community.'

He was constantly stopped by well-wishers as he paced the streets. 'It's great to see you in Cardiff,' called out one young black man. 'You have done a lot for coloured folk.'

Well yes, he conceded that the area was a slum and that the sooner a development scheme was brought in the better. 'But I have seen absolutely nothing here which compares with the District Six in Cape Town, or the shanty towns of the Reef.'

Trevor Huddlestone, the priest who battled Apartheid, visits Tiger Bay in 1957.

Then he repeated, 'Compared to them, this is paradise.'

In 1978 another visit was planned to show Trevor Huddlestone the redevelopment he'd spoken of. A welcome party was prepared, but he was forced to cancel his visit which would have included a speech at the University Hospital of Wales, because of his appointment as Bishop of Mauritius. 'But the people of Butetown have remained in my thoughts and prayers... I would have loved to have gone back there to see how the place had changed.' He never returned to the Bay, ending his days in a Yorkshire monastery.

Trevor Huddlestone was honoured throughout the world. But nowhere more than in Tiger Bay, the community which had taken him to its warm heart.

I Hereby Declare This Brothel Open...

TREVOR Huddlestone saw Tiger Bay as it neared its end. But Bute Street still retained some of its flavour, still offered echoes of those days when coal was king and the Bay was buoyant, when the pubs were packed and the girls moved in on the homeward-bounders. Let's walk down Bute Street in the last years of its pomp.

It's 1958 and the sentence of death has already been passed. But here at No. 106 is Joseph Pifaretti, ship chandler, sharing space with the Mexican consulate. Perhaps he is the Mexican consulate. Alongside them are Edward Earl and Company, ship brokers, and Jas Pridmore, coal factor. Their neighbours include more ship chandlers, marine surveyors, rope-sellers, manufacturers' agents and marine engineers. The smell of the sea rises from this old street directory speaking of a time which now seems so far away that you half expect to find the time-honoured mariners' map legend 'Here there be Dragons' printed in one corner.

At 157, Michael Eraklis, hairdresser; 159 Miss N. Lavinski, seamen's outfitter; 160, Louis Fenech, café; 163, M. Kleanthous, boot & shore repairer; 164, Cuban Café; 165, Ghana Club. And then you pass Seng Lee's Laundry and the Loudoun Hotel, and a string of cafes next door to each other, and as you walk towards town there's the Adelphi Hotel and the notorious Freemason Hotel and the Somali People's Restaurant and Zussens the Pawnshop and Hamed Hamed the grocer, next door to Jan Andullah the draper.

But what a story is recalled when you pass the Cairo Hotel, 'the boarding house for Moslem seamen.' This is something the writers of that soap *Tiger Bay* may have turned down as too improbable.

Would you believe a 16-year-old girl from Rhymney – Welsh Rhymney, not Cardiff Rumney – learning to be a nurse in the Cardiff Royal Infirmary, meeting an Arab named Ali Salaman, marrying him in 1936 when she was 16 years and three weeks old, then moving in to help him run that boarding house for Moslem seamen?

Of course you wouldn't. But long after the café had been flattened like the rest of Bute Street, Mrs Olive Salaman, once upon a time a proper little Methodist from the chapel-studded valleys, remembered those 'wonderful days'. She had swapped one culture for another, Mohammed rather than Wesley was the Prophet, and spoke Arabic with a Welsh accent. And was she ostracised by her family? Not at all. Her mother, she reminisced, 'used to love coming down to the Bay, she loved the life.' It was a time when the cafés prospered and the dice rattled on the pavement but now Bute Street is about as colourful as Cyncoed.

Olive Salaman also recalled the gambling

Mrs Olive Salaman, the girl from the valleys who came to the Bay, on Bute Street – St Mary's Church behind her – in 1957.

The famous Big Windsor Hotel when it was Mecca for gourmets from all over Britain.

houses where the Chinese gathered but for aficionadoes of old time thrillers opium is the word most associated with them. And yes, it's almost impossible to realise as you walk Bute Street today that here you once found the sort of opium den most Cardiffians thought existed only in those thrillers – in books, shall we say, like *King of Tiger Bay*. Yet one old man who was a 'telegram boy' before World War One told the *Echo* how he remembered delivering a message to a Chinese lodging house. The owner took him upstairs, 'And lo and behold, what did I see? Five Chinese sitting on the floor smoking opium. There was a bowl in the centre with tubes coming from it and they sucking. The air was thick... I was glad to get away from there.'

You still found opium dens in back rooms of Bute Street houses between the wars, When the *Echo* reflected on old Tiger Bay as it was being demolished, Harold Fowler, born in the Bay, told of rooms with bunks in them and, as part of the furniture, the opium bowl in the middle. But the main interest was gambling and down they'd come from their laundries in the valleys to play paka pu and fan tan. At one time it was rumoured

some came down from London and there were battles – 'Tong wars,' someone called them but the trouble didn't last.

It all happened in what is now a pretty placid thoroughfare. Not a pawn shop in sight where once they prospered. Anything went – clothes were bundled up on a Monday morning and 'popped' and Harold Fowler reckoned some women simply stuffed a pile of rags into a respectable-looking shirt or sheet and took them in. 'The pawnshop man knew what was going on but he also knew he'd get his money back, and he didn't want to lose a customer.'

Ask for a pawnshop around there now and they'd direct you to the Adult Sex Shop above the bridge... It's a toothless Tiger Bay these days.

But thankfully some things are left to remind us of those other days: old and beloved landmarks still survive as the the new Cardiff Bay with its imposing buildings planted over long-dead docks springs up all round. And one of them reminds us of a man who became a legend in the city's dockland. A pity that at the time of writing his shrine – for that's what it was – is no more than a sad shambles on the corner it once dominated.

But there is still a plaque on the wall of the Big Windsor and in just two dozen words it brings back, to those who know, the enchantment of an era;

'In The Difficult Days Following The War, 1939-45, ABEL MAGNERON 1890-1954 Here Achieved A Gastronomic Standard Which Contributed To The Further Glory Of The Entente Cordiale.'

Who, asked a young sixth form schoolgirl some years ago, was Abel Magneron? She had seen the plaque on the fly-postered wall of the derelict pub. Or, with due apologies to M. Magneron, L'otel. And how, she added, did the Entente Cordiale come to be mentioned. She suspected a story, and indeed there was, although it was woeful to realise that a great man, like so many others, had ended up as merely a plaque on a wall.

The man who made it a gastronomic landmark, Abel Magneron with his assistant Edmond Rey.

Abel Magneron was a chef. A French chef. Which is like saying that Picasso was a bit of a painter. Abel was an artist and his magic made a dockland public house world famous.

He leased the Big Windsor after World War Two and he, his wife Madeleine and daughter Marcelle turned it into a cullinary Mecca where worshippers assembled. He became one of the great characters of the docks, known to all as Papa. The biggest stars of, as they say, stage, screen and television, met at Papa Magneron's when appearing at the old Prince of Wales Theatre or the New Theatre or at the television and radio studios: icons like Richard Burton and Stanley Baker would down a jar or two there with sporting gods and its fame spread across the country and the continent. But Papa died in a car crash in his native France in 1954, it signalled the end, and all that's left now is the plaque commemorating his genius, provided by the Welsh aviation pioneer Kenneth Davies.

And what was that about the Entente Cordiale? Why, Papa's glorious food did more for Anglo-Welsh-French relations than any treaty ever could. Sadly, the Big Windsor was gutted by a fire in 1985 but it reopened the following year as, in the words of the new landlord, the former Cardiff rugby player John Price, 'A pub built to accom-

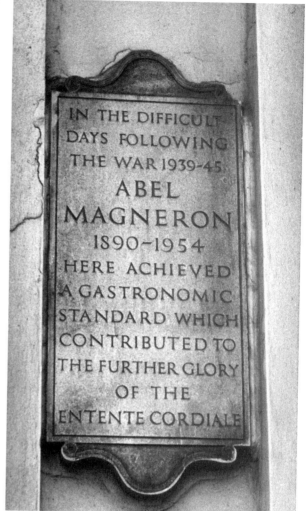

The plaque honouring the great chef outside the now dilapidated pub, placed there by admirers.

modate jazz... actually designed around a jazz bar.'

And who performed the official opening? None other than that one time docks copper Viv Brook who spent an hour on the piano. He might not have looked like Errol Flynn, someone once quipped of him, 'but he can play like Errol Garner.'

It didn't last. The Big Windsor closed again and seems to be slowly slumping into terminal decay although there are always promises... promises. The final irony is that just behind it is a symbol of

Fire at the Big Windsor in 1967 but a bigger one in 1985 gutted it.

And here's the North Star Club, long demolished, opened by James Callaghan when he was Prime Minister. The girls inside were told, 'No business tonight.'

But it reopened in 1986 with former Cardiff rugby player John Price as landlord and – who else? – Viv Brook doing the opening honours.

the New Bay – Harry Ramsden's Fish and Chip Restaurant, doing sellout business. How, you wonder, would Papa feel about that.

And have you heard the one about the Prime Minister opening a brothel?

No, Jim Callaghan didn't know about it. But it was part-owned by an active Labour Party worker with good connections and occupied space just down the road from the Packet. It rejoiced in the name the North Star Club and somehow the part-owner, another of the Bay's more memorable characters, persuaded his contacts to persuade, in turn, the Prime Minister to do the honours on the night of the official opening. It was a club in the old tradition, a former bosun of Herculean strength on the door, and a meeting place for the girls of the town who plied their trade aboard visiting ships if they could get through the dock gates. Which they often did, in the boot of a taxi. Anyway, Sunny Jim turned up and our part-owner warned the girls, 'No business tonight, this is the Prime Minister's party.' The girls behaved like a Salvation Army Choir and all went well. A flying visit by the PM and off he went.

In time the North Star Club was flattened after a compulsory purchase order and is remembered now only by nostalgic old sailors sitting at home in Bergen or Barry. And, of course, by a former Prime Minister who probably still thinks he was opening some sort of Seamen's Mission.

Some of the old pubs still remain, of course: the Ship and Pilot sits as always on its corner of Mount Stuart Square and the Bute Dock, opened in 1839 at the same time as its dock namesake, perhaps the oldest building in the area, carries on although it's now fallen prey to the trend for re-naming and is the Jug and Platter – but old timers still call it the Bute Dock.

And Now... the Tiger's Teeth Are Drawn

WHEN Trevor Huddlestone came to the Bay the signs of decline were already evident. In 1938 the docks handled some seven million tons. In 1948, after the 'artificial' figures due to the war, it was just 3.4 million tons. And in 1958, the year we walked down Bute Street, sharing the place with the shades of yesterday, it was only two million tons.

You could always measure the health of Cardiff's docks by the amount of coal shipped out. So with hindsight we could say that the tide had begun to go out as long ago as 1926 when, as we've already seen, the miners, primary source of profit over the years, stopped work, with the dockers following. They went back to a port where coal was still king. But the crown was slipping even though World War Two postponed the inevitable abdication. In 1945, James Callaghan, the new MP for Cardiff South, predicted large scale unemployment for the 4,000-odd workers. Echoing Lloyd George, he blamed the concentration on coal over the preceding 60 years, even though Cardiff had seen how it could handle general cargo during the war.

Tiger Bay in changing times. Symbolically, the twin tower block flats soar above those of St Mary's and you can see the new roads being built in 1988.

The Barrage that will transform the docks under construction.

And then, in 1948, a year when Cardiff's port trade was only 3.4 million tons, exactly half the 1938 figure, Nationalisation arrived and this was something that would have made Bill Tatem and his cronies explode. The *South Wales Echo* wasn't too happy, either. 'Nationalisation,' it pontificated, 'not only dries up previous ability to show profits but drags every nationalised industry and public utility down into insolvency.'

That dragging down was already evident. In 1946 Cardiff had handled just 3,193 ships compared to 4,241 in 1936 when only two and half per cent of exports from the port were not, as we said earlier, coal or coke or patent fuel. By 1951 the number of ships was down to 2,889 and the dockers' work force had also dwindled. But at least they now received a guaranteed wage – an innovation that would have enraged the Tatems of the old town even more.

The docks would struggle on, the export of, of all things, scrap iron rising: but that, in a way, symbolised the decline in other fields as factories and foundries were dismantled. And one of the great scrap entrepreneurs, one of the great characters, lived his last days around the docks. Cyril Clarke – Nobby to all – kept his 'office' and living quarters for a time just above Bute Street. His address, he would intone, was 'Underneath the Arches.' Nobby described himself as a company director and used a supermarket trolley to carry his stock around.

One afternoon the representative of a local supermarket appeared. 'Nobby,' he said, 'we don't mind you having the odd trolley but...' He counted. 'But you've got over a dozen here.'

'I am waiting,' replied Nobby with enormous dignity, 'for my drivers to turn up.'

He appeared one lunchtime in the Bosun,

The biggest engineering project in Welsh history.

begging for a shilling (5p) to stave off the pangs of hunger. Two ancient regulars, almost as skint, coughed up sixpence (2½p) each. Nobby changed them for a single shilling (5p) at the bar then went to the phone. Astonished, they heard him use their cash to order a taxi. Over the phone he boomed, 'From the Bosun to the Ship and Pilot.' Then, turning to his benefactors, he announced, 'You don't expect a gentleman to drink here, do you? With layabouts like you?' Nobby was in that tradition of Bay characters.

A long time ago we imagined the docks on a cinema screen, that voice over taking us back to a vibrant, pulsating port. Do the same thing now and we need the Voice, rather than a voice over – close your eyes and you can hear him singing it against a backdrop of decaying docks. Yes, Sinatra...

'And now, the end is near... and I await the final curtain.'

An ominous hint of the approach of that final curtain arrived in July 1961 when the motor vessel *Belbetty* tied up in Cardiff docks to unload the first cargo of – was that a hollow laugh we heard from the shade of old Lloyd George? – the first cargo of American coal.

And then, on 25 August 1964 we really did witness the end of an era and for once it was no cliche to say it. This is how the *South Wales Echo* began its report:

'When the coastal vessel Farringay sailed from Cardiff Docks at 6.30 am today, it wrote the last chapter in the 125 year history of the port as a coal-shipping centre.'

Just 30 or so words. But what a story they told. The last chapter in 125 years – and back we were whisked to that never-to-be-forgotten day in 1839, the day when Our Correspondent marvelled at the crowded streets, those 'merry bells of

But no arches left for Nobby, scrap entrepreneur, to conduct his business – or snooze.

death? And what of the American Consul whose toast was that 'The dock will enhance the prosperity of Cardiff as long as grass grew and water ran.' And who, on that day in 1964, remembered the *Manulus*, that 700-ton ship from Quebec, its yardarms manned by sailors shouting huzzahs.

So much had happened since 'the thrilling blasts of the Glamorganshire Band' wrenched folk from their beds on that great day which would go down in history as the day when the new Cardiff was born. It is easy to see them if you stand across from the castle today – Lord Bute and the rest emerging to march down to this spectacular new dock, the bands bravely playing, the kids scampering along until halted in mid-skip by the basilisk eye of Mr Jeremiah Stockdale, Superintendent of Police, whose name lives on in a street in Grangetown.

St John's' and at the parades and the passion and the glories yet to come. You wonder, did the shade of Our Correspondent look down with our old friend Alderman John Winstone and mourn the

Would any old timer recognise his docks today?

The world's biggest Chinese takeaway, the county headquarters on the edge of a once-crammed dock.

Since then we had said farewell to Miss Eliza Pincott and her Seminary for Young Ladies. We had watched the ghost of Cap' Tupper fade. We had gone through strikes and riots and seen Bob Downey depart along with Tommy Letton and his sister Beatrice; and we had watched Captain Scott's *Discovery* embark on its last tragic voyage and we had cheered the King and the Queen who gave her name to a dock, and their son who might, or might not have been Jack the Ripper; we had walked on to the Floor, the sacred Floor of the Exchange with Tatem and his cronies and boarded a ship with Cardiff's Blackshirts and welcomed the GIs and helped launch an invasion.

And we had seen Tiger Bay have its teeth drawn to become in all but name as much a part of the past as the Glamorganshire Band, who should have been here to play the Last Post. You die when the heart stops beating and there's no doubt that the Exchange was the heart of Cardiff docks. In April 2001, I walked into the Exchange and there,

on that fabled Floor, they were laying out tables for a function that night. This was the room where unimaginable fortunes had been made, echoing now not to the shouts of the mighty Docksmen bidding for their precious black gold, but to the clink of cutlery. The two carved lions are still perched there as they have been since Victoria reigned over another Empire, above the clock marking the morning and afternoon high tides in Cardiff, the two most significant times for those Docksmen. The legend beneath each clock should now read 'low tide' – the heart of the docks has stopped beating.

See the massive buildings, now, those vast symbols of hope in a future prosperity that would never end. Here is the National Westminster Bank, once the largest bank outside London, known as the 'Shipowners' Memorial. And there Cambrian Buildings with its echo of the great coal mining days, and Beynon House, a century ago the Baltic Buildings. What memories of Victorian

Once a place for work. Now the docks and Tiger Bay seem designed for play as the Bay hosts Wales' biggest carnival.

might do Empire House and Imperial House evoke? And so many more.

Those Docksmen owned the ego of an Ozymandius whose mighty monument was meant to last forever – 'My name is Ozymandius, King of Kings. Look on my works, ye mighty and despair.' Now, a century or so after they went up, the For Sale signs sprout, dust layers windows that have legendary docks names like John Cory inscribed into the glass. When they opened for business they must have inspired the same sort of euphoria that the new Cardiff Bay buildings bring today...

I went down to Cardiff docks in January 1965, to write what really amounted to an obituary. Not of the docks themselves – although it was never clear then what the future would bring. This was, in a way, a farewell to the docks that Bute had dreamed of and, in the end, had made reality. Here is the opening paragraph of that report filed when the docks looked to become as much a part of the past as Byzantium or Troy:

'The Mount Stuart Hotel squats, scowling, opposite the gates leading into Cardiff's vast docks. The lounge has been closed; the luncheon bar no longer sags beneath pyramids of meat pies and thick beef wedges; there is room in the public bar for anyone who feels inclined to expose himself to the tangible chill that permeates the air. The days when, it was said, the barmaids swept up five hundredweights of coaldust after every rowdy session, after every gathering of dust-choked coal-trimmers, have gone. There are no coal-trimmers

And there are also free concerts in the Bay.

on Cardiff's docks today and, the locals sigh, there are not really any docks any more.'

No coal-trimmers... once there had been 2,700 but on that day there were only 150 along the entire coast, concentrated in two surviving docks at Barry and Swansea. No coal-trimmers: no coal. Yet once, I mused as I walked those desolate docks, once the great grey fleets of the world had devoured Welsh steam coal and anthracite as fast as it could be mined and exported. Bunker stations across the globe, black monuments to Britain's colonial might, were kept at mountain size. And all because of these docks.

As always there were optimists along at the Chamber of Commerce. Money would still be made, they said. No, not through exports: what was there to export? But into the docks would come oil and iron ore and grain. The vision, then, was still of a working docks rather than the massive commercial and leisure centre it's since become.

On that day in the Mount Stuart, Billy Westlake, 50 years on the docks, summed up his feelings, and, maybe, the feelings of all those who had worked those docks since the Manulus began it all in 1839.

'But it's not like coal. Coal was different. It was... well, like it was ours. Coming from Wales to go right across the world. Physically they might be able to do something, but the soul of the docks has gone forever.'

Well, that was said on a day in January 1965 when men like Billy Westlake were still numbed by the thought that the last coal had left Cardiff, the city built on coal.

That year they closed the West Dock and in time it was filled in and the grass that David Davies had promised so long ago began to grow on it. The East Dock was sealed off ten years later while they ripped up the railway sidings and began to plan for the future. Up went the headquarters of the Glamorgan County Council, a huge pagoda-style building referred to by the irreverent as the biggest Chinese takeaway in Britain. Dock landmarks like the Spillers flour mill were converted into apartments while the LMS warehouse was transforrmed into the Celtic Bay Hotel. Houses mushroomed in what is now called Atlantic Wharf and officialdom spread the notion that here in Cardiff we had a sort of Little Venice. And now we have the Bute Town carnival and concerts where once Shanghai Walsh roamed, bands playing on the ribbon of grass that marks the path of the canal, hot dog vendors in place of the cafes and pubs that once made every day a carnival.

Miss Eliza Pincott might have approved but for those dyed-in-the-wool Bay boys and the lads from the Docks it was the end. They feel that there will be no room for them in the bright Bay of the 21st century, that the Diaspora will come and they will end up in Cardiff's outer reaches as so many before them. The new road where their old Bute Street ran from the city centre to the docks is to be called Lloyd George Boulevard. Ironic, eh? To name the main thoroughfare of the new docks after the man who prophesied the end of the old docks.

The Barrage, as revolutionary a project in its impact on the city as Bute's first dock, runs from the Queen's Dock to Penarth Head, blocking out that sea with its 40-foot tides, bringing instead a 500-acre freshwater lake (they say) instead of mudflats. New roads, tunnels, sprouting buildings

But artist John Allinson has ensured that the scenes of old Tiger Bay and the docks will not be forgotten. He sits in front of a docks scene...

– all come together to make those old docks unrecognisable.

Thankfully, though, those old Docks and the Bay and some of those beloved old characters who walked them, and the places where they talked and drank and dreamed have been preserved. Walk into the Baltimore Hotel and there they are, brought vividly back to life by the huge talent of John Allinson, whose murals resurrect the pulsating past of the Docks and Tiger Bay. John himself kept a bar next to the empty space where the much-mourned Mount Stuart once stood and from this vantage point he fell in love with a disappearing dockland he felt he had to honour.

So, through his marvellous art in pubs and restaurants and at times on the streets themselves, you get a glimpse of what once was. And the men and women who packed the past with passion and

...while here are some of his paintings on the bar in the Baltiomore Hotel, his murals fill the walls and ceilings as well.

pride and fighting and fun live on, looking down from walls and ceilings, down on to another generation for whom the Docks and the Bay John Allinson celebrates are no more than myth.

Buffs – Mount Stuart Square by John Allinson.

But Time's wheel turns and here we are at the beginning of a new era. When it seems that the colour and the character have faded along with those giants of the past like Tatem and Tupper, Father Purveau, Bob Downey, Shanghai Walsh and all the rest. Perhaps in another hundred years someone will write of this new era as the beginning of another Golden Age at Cardiff docks while the citizens of Cardiff who remember will look back and muse that the place has lost its charm. If, of course, the Bay by then isn't buried by water like some miniature Atlantis.

We'll never know. All we can do is look back at what really *was* a Golden Age,

And, if you knew those docks and Tiger Bay as they were, you'll maybe mourn, and wonder if the next epoch won't be so much gold as gold-plated.

One thing's for sure. For a lad savouring his green years the Mystic East will no longer begin at Cardiff's Clarence bridge.

But they can never take the place of the beloved Mount Stuart Hotel. And here is old docker Mike Kenefick ('Where's yer kilt?') with his mate Danny Sexton, supping a last pint of the pub's legendary SA before it's demolished.

Index